BROLLIOLOGY

BROLLIOLOGY

A HISTORY OF THE UMBRELLA IN LIFE AND LITERATURE

MARION RANKINE

MELVILLE HOUSE UK

LONDON

BROLLIOLOGY

Copyright © 2017 by Marion Rankine

First Melville House Printing: November 2017

Melville House Publishing   8 Blackstock Mews
              46 John Street   and   Islington
        Brooklyn, NY 11201   London N4 2BT

mhpbooks.com   facebook.com/mhpbooks   @melvillehouse

ISBN: 978-1-61219-670-1

Printed in China
1 3 5 7 9 10 8 6 4 2

Design by Marina Drukman

A catalog record for this book is available from the Library of Congress

for Big Dog

and the Brolly Hunters

UNDERGROUND

MANNER

NO WET · NO COLD

Contents

BROLLIOLOGY

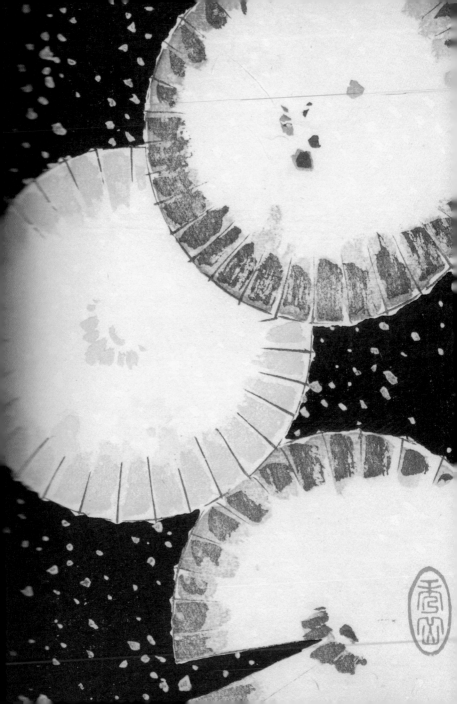

Introduction ‖ BROLLYNESS

WHAT CAN GO up a chimney down, but can't go down a chimney up? Of all the childhood riddles I picked up in my first few years of school, this one has stuck with me the longest. Perhaps it was the absurdity of anyone wanting to thread an umbrella through a chimney that tickled me, or the enduring image of open umbrellas making mushrooms of chimney pots (we had a chimney, and the temptation to stick an umbrella in its top was not inconsiderable). Or maybe it was the realization that umbrellas, like flowers, have two states of being—furled and open—of which each state is mutually exclusive. A rolled-up umbrella may serve as a walking stick; an open one certainly won't. Likewise, a closed umbrella is of no assistance whatsoever when the clouds open—save in its potential to flower. What other common object enacts such a radical visual transformation when we put it to use?

This everyday act of transformation is, I believe, part of the charm of "umbrellaness" (or to adapt the British vernacular: "brollyness.") And charm it undoubtedly is, for humans have been making,

OPPOSITE: *Bijutsu Kai [Ocean of Art]*. Night, snow and umbrellas collide in this beautiful Japanese print from the early twentieth century

using, perfecting and decorating umbrellas for millennia. Umbrellas have been held over the heads of rulers, chieftains, kings, queens, priests, gods, nobles, revelers, clergymen, merchants, monks, clerks and lovers. They have been crafted from bamboo, paper, whalebone, steel, silk, cotton, alpaca, brocade and lace, and trimmed with jewels and precious metals. Umbrellas have appeared in countless movies and artwork for their sheer aesthetic appeal and their ability to create points of calm amidst pelting rain or swirling snow.

Umbrellas have also been written about: extensively, revealingly, delightfully. A couple of enthusiasts (one of them a famous umbrella-maker of his time) have even written histories of the object. Others have slipped umbrellas into their narratives the same way umbrellas slip in and out of our notice in everyday life: subtly, mostly; symbolically, often; and, occasionally, in life-changing, plot-altering ways.

Some years ago I was seized by the idea of writing about umbrellas in literature. My thought, at the time, was to write an essay: a brief tour of some of my favourite literary umbrellas, with a few notes on their function within the narrative. However, as I started to read around the subject, and delved into the history of umbrellas in cultures from ancient Egypt to present-day Britain, I swiftly realized that an essay would not suffice. The history of umbrellas is deep and far-reaching, and the meanings and symbolism attached to them vary wildly from century to century and place to place. The more I read, the more trails I found to other books, other angles, perspectives and dimensions. Odd though my subject was, it was spilling over the edges of any small form I tried to contain it in.

I came to realize that what I was attempting was not a catalogue of umbrellas in English-language literature.[1] Such a study would be immense (to take just one author as an example, there are over 120 references to umbrellas in the work of Charles Dickens

---

[1] Warren Motte's *Mirror Gazing* (2014) is a fantastic example of literary collecting—in this case, of "mirror scenes," in which characters encounter themselves in reflection. Motte's book is built on over twenty-five years of reading, making it both diverse and astoundingly comprehensive.

alone[2])—and, I believe, contrary to the spirit of what was emerging from my ever-lengthening notes. After all, I wasn't simply fascinated with umbrellas in literature—my interest lay rather with *ideas* of umbrellaness, both in the "real" world and the fictional, conceptual universes contained within books. It was not the objects themselves—beautiful as they may be—that fascinated me, but the meanings behind them.

There are many facets of brollyness, and as I examined each one I found their reflections, or corollaries, in the literary examples collecting in drifts on my study floor. The way we write about things naturally reveals how we think about them and the meanings we attach to them, and the way we write about umbrellas is no exception. I read about umbrellas that are assiduously remembered, others that are forgotten; umbrellas wielded aggressively and umbrellas wielded meekly; umbrellas that disrupt convention and others that uphold it; umbrellas that protect and umbrellas that wound; umbrellas that betray more about a character's social standing than any other element in the narrative and umbrellas without which the narrative would not have been possible. The more I read about umbrellas, the more I became convinced that these objects occupy the very opposite of an everyday role in our reading: they are variously magical, comical, (dis)functional, (im)practical, invasive, liminal, and in all cases, indispensable.

This is a book that will never—could never—be complete. In the last days of cobbling together a final first draft, a colleague told me his favourite literary brolly was from *Madame Bovary*. *Madame Bovary?* In all my literary umbrella research, Flaubert had not surfaced once. I ran to the local Oxfam bookshop on my lunch break to pick up a copy, and it spent a few months sitting by my bedside, patiently awaiting inclusion in the second draft. No doubt the experience will repeat itself. From my own small journeyings through the

---

2   This figure comes from John Bowen's wonderful essay "Dickens's Umbrellas" (2013)—a true paean to the literary powers of both Dickens and the brolly.

wealth of books in the world, I have encountered enough umbrellas to be certain that—like stars in the universe and strange creatures of the deepest seas—far more await discovery than are already known. But the specimens you will encounter in the following pages remain dear to me, for they built this book and revealed myriad meanings to be found in the humble brolly.

1 ‖ MARKS OF DISTINCTION

O N T H E V E H I C L E - C H O K E D intersection of New Oxford and Bloomsbury streets in London, opposite a souvenir shop decked in monarchial tat and sprouting with cheap umbrellas on rainy days, a quick walk from a greasy spoon in one direction and the cobbled laneways of Covent Garden in the other, stands an anachronism. The creamy Victorian façade of Hazelwood House is emblazoned with red lettering and wrought-iron decorations, a relic of advertising from the days before overlarge photographs and swiftly changing window displays. A sign swings off an ornate iron support: JAMES SMITH & SONS UMBRELLAS. The words are capped with a broad red canopy—deprived of its stick but nonetheless quintessential. The text bordering the glass windows proclaims a range of products: Ladies' Umbrellas; Tropical Sunshades; Garden & Golf Umbrellas; Gentlemen's Umbrellas; Fox Frames; Gold & Silver Mounters; Umbrellas Recovered, Renovated & Repaired; Sticks Repolished; Riding Crops & Whips; Fresh Blackthorns; Malacca Canes; Life Preservers; Dagger Canes; Swordsticks . . .

Venture inside the tiny shop and you're met with profusions of dark wood and wicker, canopies tight-furled or casually ruffled, slack tartan, sleek walking sticks, and bouquets of ladies' umbrellas displayed in stands, stems curving elegantly upward. Ducks, parrots, poodles, greyhounds, boxers, Scotties, crocodiles, toucans, rams, billiard balls, Sherlock Holmes and Beethoven stare stonily out from racks of hand-carved walking sticks, and everywhere else the ubiquitous hooked handles make staccato rhythms across the room. High on the walls, solemn pairs of antlers—branching elk and corkscrew eland—add to the air of upper-class dignity.

As much a tourist attraction as the nearby British Museum or the proliferation of theatres just a few blocks south, James Smith & Sons stands as a testament to the enduring power of the brolly in the British imagination—more specifically, to the brolly as a carefully crafted sign of high distinction, to be carried not only as a shield against the wet, but as a mark of fashion and good taste. "We can happily estimate the value of such a friend as the Umbrella, the silent companion of our walks abroad," William Sangster, umbrella-maker, rhapsodized in 1855, and just a few minutes in James Smith & Sons may well convince you of the sound logic of his feelings.

James Smith & Sons was founded in 1830—a notable date, for it was around this time, according to umbrella historian T. S. Crawford, that umbrella manufacture became a commercially viable prospect. Indeed, the 1830s was a key decade for fashion in general. In *Victorian Fashion Accessories* (2012) fashion historian Ariel Beaujot identifies two important factors that shaped the course of British history: the "solidification" of the middle class and the resulting increase in consumption. Luxury objects that had previously been the preserve of the ultrarich were democratized through the production of cheaper, but still high quality, imitations, and flaunted as signs of status and refinement. The middle class used these objects to demonstrate their difference from the working class; more specifically, women used them to show off their husband's income. Where the act of lavishing money on frivolous objects had once been seen as morally corrupt—another preserve of the aristou crats—it was increasingly viewed as advantageous to society by supb porting production and providing employment for workers.

This democratization was reflected in umbrella-related develm opments: street-corner hawkers were replaced by family firms and small manufacturers as the demand for umbrellas skyrocketed. The heavy, fragile whalebone frames used in earlier designs were gradually replaced—in what Sangster hailed as "the greatest improvement yet introduced in the manufacture of an Umbrella"—by Mr Fox's Paragon frame, a lightweight steel construction inspired by the architecture of a bridge.[3] In 1851 William Sangster and his brother John were awarded a prize at the Great Exhibition of 1851 for their pioneering use of alpaca (or "Peruvian sheep," as Sangster called it) fabric as a substitute for the hitherto-used silk and cotton covers, which were expensive (silk), unwieldy (cotton), and not satisfactorily durable (both). By 1855 they had sold nearly four million of their Fox-framed, alpaca-canopied articles.

The umbrella had firmly established itself as a mark of distinction.[4] "Its possession," writes Robert Louis Stevenson in a pert little essay called "The Philosophy of Umbrellas" (1894), "implies a certain comfortable provision of fortune . . . it is the habitual carriage of the umbrella that is the stamp of Respectability. The umbrella has become the acknowledged index of social position." In his 1907 travel narrative *Wild Wales*, George Borrow writes:

> [W]ho doubts that you are a respectable character provided
> you have an umbrella? You go into a public-house and
> call for a pot of beer, and the publican puts it down before
> you with one hand, without holding out the other for the
> money, for he sees that you have an umbrella and conse-

---

3 Specifically, a tubular bridge called the Britannia Bridge, built over the Menai Strait by Robert Stephenson. The bridge was rebuilt (and tubularity abandoned) following a fire in 1970.

4 For more on when it wasn't considered such a mark of distinction, see Chapter 2.

A 1901 advertisement for Fox's umbrella-frames (fox presumably not included)

quently property. And what respectable man, when you overtake him on the way and speak to him, will refuse to hold conversation with you, provided you have an umbrella? No one. The respectable man sees that you have an umbrella and concludes that you do not intend to rob him, and with justice, for robbers never carry umbrellas. Oh, a tent, a shield, a lance and a voucher for character is an umbrella. Amongst the very best of friends of man must be reckoned an umbrella.

By Borrow's time the umbrella had well and truly worked its way into the British dress code. Gentlemen typically equipped themselves with a "city umbrella"—what Crawford describes as a "tightly-rolled and immaculate silk-clad stick which served as scepter to the bowler hat's crown."

Crawford does not reference crowns and scepters lightly. In fact, umbrellas have a long history of distinction far predating the British. More than three thousand years ago, they were held over monarchs for sun protection in ancient Egypt as well as in ancient Assyria. Charles Dickens (possibly the most avid brolliologist of literary history) published an essay on umbrellas in his weekly magazine, *Household Words*, in which he refers to a Theban image depicting an Ethiopian princess "traveling in a car, to which is attached an umbrella or sun-shade, bearing a strong resemblance to the chaise umbrella which Mr and Mrs Smith take out with them on their Sunday's ride to Epping Forest."

Traveling in the former kingdom of Dahomey (now Benin), Sir Richard Burton observed in 1966 that each new chief was given an umbrella, "which was figuratively used to denote the chief himself, 'seven umbrellas have fallen' meaning seven chiefs had been killed." Ethiopia, Morocco, and West Africa were known for their use of stately umbrellas—particularly Morocco, where for centuries only the ruler and his immediate family were permitted to carry one. An

This detail from an Ajanta Cave fresco shows a woman being shaded with a long-stemmed umbrella

old Moroccan saying hints at the luxury afforded by the object: "The owner of an umbrella goes as it pleases him, in the sun or in the shade."

Ancient frescos from the Ajanta Caves (second century B.C.E.–550 C.E.) reflect the long and distinguished history enjoyed by the umbrella in India. As in many countries, umbrellas were mostly associated with kingship. In 1905 Samuel Purchas wrote of the Great Mogul, "of kittasols[5] of state, for to shadow him, there be twenty. None in his empire dareth in any sort have any of these carried for his shadow but him." Only monarchs (and even then, only on special occasions) were permitted to use the *nava-danda*: a seven-tiered parasol of scarlet and gold dressed in thirty-two strings of pearls, with a pure gold frame, ruby handle and diamond knob. Cochin rajahs required postage stamps to include an outline of an umbrella.

When the Prince of Wales visited India in 1887, he was shaded at all times with a massive umbrella—less for protection against the heat than for the strength of association between umbrellas and sovereignty in the minds of the Indian people. As Ariel Beaujot explains, without the umbrella Prince Edward may simply have been taken for "an unimportant Western visitor rather than the future emperor of their nation."

In Burma, the king of the ancient capital Ava was called "King of

---

5   *Kittasol* is a variation of *quitasol*, the Spanish word for "sunshade."

the White Elephants and Lord of the Twenty-Four Umbrellas." One thirteenth-century monarch chose his successor by arranging his five sons in a circle and letting an umbrella drop between them, praying that it would fall towards the most deserving. According to Crawford, the resultant royal, Prince Oksana, was known as "the king whom the umbrella placed on the throne."

In China, evidence of umbrella use goes back millennia. Collapsible umbrella stays were discovered in the tomb of warlord Wang Kuang, dated to 25 B.C.E.—a fact which might have humbled eighteenth-century British umbrella-makers wrestling with similar technologies. In the Ming Dynasty (1368–1644), an extraordinarily detailed system of class-based umbrella etiquette was in practice: the governor-

Ornate and betasseled, this Indian state umbrella boasts
exquisite craftsmanship and a silver stem

general carried two large red silk umbrellas; the four highest mann darins carried black models with a red silk lining and three flounces; the lesser nobility were permitted two flounces; gentlemen commoners of two highest ranks had red umbrellas with a gourd-shaped knob of tin; the following two ranks of gentlemen had the same but with a wooden knob painted red; and the fifth rank of gentlemen had a blue cloth umbrella with two flounces and a red-painted knob. "Common" people were not allowed umbrellas covered in cloth or silk and had to make do with sturdy paper umbrellas instead.

In Japan, complicated rules about colour and rank likewise dictated umbrella use amongst the nobility until the late seventeenth century, when well-off city dwellers began carrying *wagasa*—thin paper-and-bamboo umbrellas lacquered against the rain. These became immensely popular until Western umbrellas started appearing in the late nineteenth century. Their enduring popularity was such that traditional umbrella-making became a dying craft.[6]

Back in Victorian Britain, the umbrella reached such heights of popularity that it was even carried into battle. After one clash during the Napoleonic Wars, according to Crawford, "the ground was covered with sabers, satchels and umbrellas." This elicited no little bemusement from the French. One marshal wrote:

> It was raining and the English officers were on horseback,
> each with an umbrella in hand, which seemed to me eminently ridiculous. All at once the English closed their
> umbrellas, hung them on their saddles, drew their sabers,
> and threw themselves upon our Chausseurs.

---

6   For the curious, Stephan Köhler's 1993 essay "Parents of Private Skies" (from Julia Meech's *Rain and Snow: The Umbrella in Japanese Art*)—traces the construction of traditional umbrellas from craftsperson to craftsperson in Gifu City. The umbrella-making processes are exacting, exquisite and performed almost entirely by elderly craftspeople—a fact that, over two decades later, makes for bittersweet reading.

Reports from the battlefield had apparently not reached Robert Louis Stevenson, who opined in "The Philosophy of Umbrellas" that possession of an umbrella ought to signal a degree of pacifism in its owner, owing to their judicious protection of so valuable an article:

> One who bears with him an umbrella—such a complicated structure of whalebone, of silk, and of cane, that it becomes a very microcosm of modern industry—is necessarily a man of peace. A half-crown cane may be applied to an offender's head on a very moderate provocation; but a six-and-twenty shilling silk is a possession too precious to be adventured in the shock of war.

One anecdote holds that when the Duke of Cambridge found some much-needed shelter beneath an expansive canopy, his troops burst into song:

> *We don't want to fight,*
> *But by Jingo, if we do,*
> *We've got the Duke of Cambridge*
> *And his umbrella too!*

In an age when an umbrella can now be got for the price of a pint, and left behind, without regret, after one too many, it can be easy to forget the value once invested in the object. It takes a character like Leonard Bast, the clerk in E. M. Forster's 1910 novel *Howard's End*, to remind us. Leonard has the misfortune of having his umbrella taken during a concert, and finds himself quite unable to concentrate without it:

> [H]e could not quite forget about his stolen umbrella. Yes, the umbrella was the real trouble. Behind Monet and Debussy the umbrella persisted, with the steady beat of a

drum. "I suppose my umbrella will be all right," he was thinking. "I don't really mind about it. I will think about music instead. I suppose my umbrella will be all right."

Or Mary Poppins, whose umbrella accompanies her on adventure after adventure with the Banks children—whether it's raining or not.

> Mary Poppins put on her white gloves and tucked her umbrella under her arm—not because it was raining but because it had such a beautiful handle that she couldn't possibly leave it at home. How could you leave your umbrella behind if it had a parrot's head for a handle?

In Roald Dahl's short story "The Umbrella Man" (1980), a mother and daughter visiting London are caught in a sudden rainstorm. An elderly man, with all the appearance of being a "real gentleman" approaches them on the street: "He was polite. He was well-spoken. He was well-dressed." Moreover, he is carrying an enormous silk umbrella, worth at least £20. Nevertheless, the mother is suspicious, particularly when he informs her that he's left his wallet at home and he needs a fare for the taxi home. Her suspicions wilt when he offers her his umbrella in exchange for £1:

> "It's a lovely umbrella," the little man said.
> "So I've noticed," my mother said.
> "It's silk," he said.
> "I can see that."

Here, the little man's umbrella is invested with such value that it acts as a currency, both social and economic. The high quality of the umbrella grants Stevenson's "stamp of respectability"—a guaran-

OPPOSITE: Prince George, Duke of Cambridge, caricatured with his eminent umbrella

tee of character and social standing—thereby ensuring that the old gentleman's advances will be favourably received and his proposed transaction accepted with good grace.

A similar valuation of an umbrella appears in George Herbert Rodwell's *Memoirs of an Umbrella* (1847). Here, the gifting of an umbrella is a significant enough act to raise suspicions of hidden motives, when Herbert Trevillian, a morally corrupt gentleman of high social standing, attempts to secure the affections of a new acquaintance, Mr Stutters—who immediately sees through him: "His begging as a favour, that I would keep that umbrella as my own, when I merely sent to ask the loan of it. Trifle as it is, it shows a desire to lay me under an obligation."

The worth of an umbrella, and its role in signaling social status, is given a thorough airing in art critic Brian Sewell's only novel, *The White Umbrella* (2015). Mr B, an affable and slightly barmy English gent of scholarly pursuits and apparent financial boundlessness, takes it upon himself to rescue an immature, mistreated donkey from the streets of Peshawar. In doing so, he abandons the television crew he is supposed to be filming with and opts instead to return to his comfortable Wimbledon home by foot, car, truck, train and any other transport that will safely convey a young donkey. He clings to his umbrella through the entire journey. After all, it is

> no ordinary umbrella, but one of strong white canvas on a frame of metal ribs exquisitely engineered about a stock as heavy as the strongest walking-stick, specially made for him ten years before . . . by James Smith & Sons . . . The canvas was no longer white, for this was an umbrella that had crossed the Sahara and its sand-storms when Mr B was searching there for evidence of prehistoric human occupation, that had been with him in Pompeii and furthest Sicily, indeed everywhere from Barcelona to Baghdad, and had proved to be the Rolls-Royce of umbrellas.

In Mr B's hands, the white umbrella comes to serve many narrative purposes. As it turns out, most of these have more to do with signaling his status as a wealthy English gentleman than with keeping the sun off Pavlova—the donkey—and himself. Throughout the arduous journey, only his umbrella saves him from the indignity of looking poor: he "felt like a tramp; unwashed, he was as grubby as a tramp; and only the cut of his clothes and the magnificence of his umbrella prevented his being mistaken for a tramp."

However, as the story progresses, we begin to wonder whether Mr B would have been wiser to have left his expensive umbrella behind. A driver gives the struggling pair a lift across a difficult section of road, and in the course of their conversation makes it clear that he understands Mr B to be English. Mr B asks how the driver knew. "It's the umbrella," he laughs, and the reader senses a delicate parallel between the umbrella's whiteness and that of Mr B's skin. As it happens, the driver is a smuggler, using the unwitting Mr B as cover for his operation. Later, a new friend tells Mr B that he, "an Englishman with money in [his] pocket—for [his] splendid umbrella makes that obvious," is "lucky to be alive."

The passage directly equates umbrellas with a fair measure of personal wealth. Given their historical entanglement with dynasties of monarchs and aristocrats, it's not surprising that umbrellas came to carry a payload of class connotations.

Nowhere in literature are the umbrella's class associations more painfully obvious than in *Howard's End*. Midway through the aforementioned concert, (the wealthy) Helen Schlegel finds herself overwhelmed by a performance of Beethoven and decides to leave early, absentmindedly taking (the not-at-all-wealthy) Leonard Bast's umbrella on her way out. Leonard has only just met Helen, and cannot help but think her behaviour deliberate. Despite her most fervent reassurances, Helen's sister Margaret is met with cold reserve when she tries to get Leonard's address in order to return the umbrella:

[T]his fool of a young man thought that she and Helen . . . had been playing the confidence trick on him, and that if he gave his address they would break into his rooms some midnight or other and steal his walking-stick too. Most ladies would have laughed, but Margaret really minded, for it gave her a glimpse into squalor. To trust people is a luxury in which only the wealthy can indulge; the poor cannot afford it. As soon as Brahms had grunted himself out, she gave him her card and said: "That is where we live; if you preferred, you could call for the umbrella after the concert, but I didn't like to trouble you when it has all been our fault."

As it happens, Leonard Bast does prefer to collect it himself. As he walks back with Margaret and her brother, Tibby, the gulf between them, first opened by the umbrella, yawns still wider to encompass beauty, culture and refinement, as Margaret's discourses on literature and art and music reveal the inequalities in their respective educations and free time:

Her speeches fluttered away from the young man like birds. If only he could talk like this, he would have caught the world. Oh, to acquire culture! Oh, to pronounce foreign names correctly! Oh, to be well-informed, discoursing at ease on every subject that a lady started! But it would take one years. With an hour at lunch and a few shattered hours in the evening, how was it possible to catch up with leisured women, who had been reading steadily from childhood?

Back at the Schlegels' house, Leonard Bast, devastated at the potential loss of one umbrella, must witness Helen joking carelessly about theft, so rich in umbrellas that she does not even know which is hers:

"Oh, I am so sorry!" cried Helen . . . "I do nothing but steal umbrellas. I am so very sorry! Do come in and choose one. Is yours a hooky or a nobbly? Mine's a nobbly—at least, I think it is."

The light was turned on, and they began to search the hall, Helen . . . commenting with shrill little cries . . .

"What about this umbrella?" She opened it. "No, it's all gone along the seams. It's an appalling umbrella. It must be mine."

But it was not.

Leonard Bast's umbrella—besides occasioning the entire plot of the novel—comes to stand for all that separates him (lower middle class, longing for education and art and time in which to pursue both) from the Schlegels (wealthy in all three and troubled only by the "goblin footfall" of his visit), the reminder that

> all is not for the best in the best of all possible worlds, and that beneath these superstructures of wealth and art there wanders an ill-fed boy, who has recovered his umbrella indeed, but who has left no address behind him, and no name.

From this single interaction disaster ensues, in part resulting from the Schlegels' solicitude for Leonard's welfare; in part from the sad truth that

> [i]n [Bast's] day the angel of Democracy had arisen, enshadowing the classes with leathern wings, and proclaiming, "All men are equal—all men, that is to say, who possess umbrellas . . ."

But—as Leonard Bast's "appalling" accessory hints—even those men who do possess umbrellas are not equal. Ariel Beaujot's extensive research into nineteenth-century British umbrella culture reveals that even amongst umbrella-possessing men, a clear hierarchy remained. The black "city umbrella" may have been available for (almost) all to use, but social differences could, nevertheless, instantly reveal themselves in the make and condition of said umbrellas. Generally, silk umbrellas were the preserve of aristocrats; lower classes had to content themselves with cotton (or the aforementioned Peruvian sheep). The material of the handle likewise indicated the extent of a gentleman's disposable income. How often a person could afford to have their umbrella recovered was evident in the condition of the fabric and the state of its seams.

Even the way an umbrella was rolled was considered indicative of a person's social standing. Silk rolled more neatly than the cheaper, bulkier cotton alternative, and a whole host of undesirable character traits were attributed to those unfortunate brolly-bearers who did not fold their accessories correctly. Herbert Howard, author of a 1900 magazine article called "Can You Fold Your Umbrella?" lists a few: "untidiness, lack of method, finnicking nicety, hurry, temper . . . carelessness." Sangster & Co. even printed instructions on the proper aristocratic rolling of an umbrella, to spare customers the indignity of such judgments.

Far (very far) from the class and civility of a properly rolled silk umbrella is one painstakingly fashioned on a blindingly hot island by literature's most famous castaway. When Robinson Crusoe, eponymous hero of Daniel Defoe's 1719 novel, becomes marooned on an (apparently) uninhabited island, he sets about fashioning various articles necessary to his survival—one of which is an umbrella. To Robert Louis Stevenson, Crusoe's umbrella is evidence of the "hankering after [umbrellas] inherent in the civilised and educated mind." He continues:

> To the superficial, the hot suns of Juan Fernandez may
> sufficiently account for his quaint choice of a luxury; but

Impeccably rolled and ruffled, with a price tag to match:
umbrellas in The Pen Shoppe, Brisbane

surely one who had borne the hard labour of a seaman
under the tropics for all these years could have supported
an excursion after goats or a peaceful *constitutional* arm
in arm with the nude Friday. No, it was not this: the
memory of a vanished respectability called for some out-
ward manifestation, and the result was—an umbrella. A
pious castaway might have rigged up a belfry and solaced
his Sunday mornings with the mimicry of church-bells;
but Crusoe was rather a moralist than a pietist, and his

leaf-umbrella is as fine an example of the civilised mind
striving to express itself under adverse circumstances as
we have ever met with.

Crusoe's umbrella was fashioned of animal hide, not leaves, and
the suggestion that such a heavy, unwieldy, and rank-smelling object
could, on that remote island, have conveyed even an echo of civili-
zation and respectability somewhat stretches credibility. But in any
case I doubt that Stevenson's tongue ventured terribly far from his
cheek throughout the writing of this essay.[7] He does, however, have
an unlikely supporter in, of all places, contemporary fiction. Gilbert
Cook, ardent socialist and Audrey Death's lover in Will Self's
novel *Umbrella* (2012), makes exactly the same point: "[W]hen
Crushoe—that quinteshenshial petit-bourgeois—is cashtaway, the
firsht implement that he makesh for himshelf ish an umbrella!"
Whatever his motivations for fashioning one, Crusoe's umbrella
made such an impression on the reading public that it entered the
vernacular, and—for a time—"robinson" become a popular term
for the umbrella.

Gilbert Cook's observations on the petit-bourgeois-ness of umbrellas are not so far from Forster's regarding the "angel of Democracy"—
and are more than borne out by the conditions of umbrella manufacture
in existence at the time, which created a clear class division between
those who carried umbrellas and those who made them. In his essay
"Umbrellas," Charles Dickens wrote extensively of the cost in human
labour occasioned in the crafting of one single umbrella—a passage
which I will quote at length, for it affords a fascinating glimpse into
preindustrial umbrella manufacture.

---

7 His parting note: "This paper was written in collaboration with James Waiter Ferrier,
   and if reprinted this is to be stated, though his principal collaboration was to lie back
   in an easy-chair and laugh."

The workman receives stick, ribs, stretchers, and runners from the warehouse; he provides iron wire and sheet brass; his workshop is supplied at his own charge with lathes, saws, rose-cutters, drills, paring-knives, a vice, pliers, and other tools; and he and his lads—two to four in number—set to work. First, the stick goes through its prescribed ordeal; . . . twisted about the while . . . The workers taper one end for receiving the ferule; they cut two grooves for receiving the two springs which respectively keep the umbrella closed and open; they insert the springs in these grooves, they adjust a stopper of wire to prevent the slides from going too far, and they fix a cross wire with a staple at each end of it.

Thus much for the stick; and now for the ribs. The workman and his staff of boys roughly taper the slip of whalebone which is to form a rib; they shape it, and smooth it, and varnish its tip; they drill a hole in it, to facilitate the fastening to the cover; they shape and smooth the head, lap sheet brass around it, and drill a hole through it for the bit of wire which is afterwards to form a hinge; they similarly drill and shield it at the middle point where the stretcher is to be fastened, and they attach it to the stretcher by means of a little axis of wire. When all the eight ribs have been doctored in this way, they are separately weighed or weighted; that is, they are tested in respect to strength and flexibility, in order that the eight for any one umbrella may be selected as nearly equally as possible: a necessary condition for the symmetrical set of the umbrella when open. Thus far done, the busy workers proceed to thread the ribs; they insert a bit of wire in a drilled hole in each stretcher; they fasten the stretcher to a notch in the slides by means of this wire, and they fasten the ribs to their meeting point by other pieces of wire.

An extraordinary amount of labour, and Dickens describes the three farthings paid for each frame as "scarcely credible."[8] A workk man and his four assistants could produce nearly six hundred of these frames in a week, for which the workman would receive up to six hundred pence[9]—eight shillings of which would have been spent on his iron wire and sheet brass.[10] On the brolly-makers' almost total lack of profit, Dickens reflects, "When the next shower of rain imW pels us to open an umbrella, let us look at its skeleton, and ponder on the amount of labour rendered for a penny or twopence."[11]

Half a century later, in Audrey Death's London, similar drudg- ery is occasioned by the putting together of umbrellas for Thomas Ince & Coy. The factory workers

> cut the silk and gingham, oil it, stretch it, sew the fin- icky loops and sleeves, then feed in the ribs and attach the handle . . . Over and over they do it . . . hands *chapped and chafed*, covered with bunions in winter . . . [italics in original][12]

Umbrellas, when used abroad, went a step further than class di- mensions: in many places they evinced the gross inequalities of colo- nialism and clashes in cultural meaning-making. In the slave markets of Goa, umbrellas were carried by Europeans. "Doubtless some pro- tection from the sun was necessary," brolly historian T. S. Crawford admits, "but the colonists obviously had adopted umbrellas as status symbols, Goa being a paradise for the parvenu where most of the work

---

8   Some unscientific fiddling with online currency and inflation calculators yields a figure of around £0.34 in today's terms—"scarcely credible" indeed!

9   Equivalent to £285 today.

10 Equivalent to £46 today.

11 Equivalent to between £0.24 and £0.48 today.

12 For the sake of tidiness, this disclaimer applies to all future quotations from Self's *Umbrella*.

was done by slaves." Near Lake Tanganyika in 1875, Commander
V. L. Cameron observed an African man carrying an umbrella:

> I was greatly amused by one of the guides who displayed
> much pride at possessing an umbrella. He kept it open for
> the whole day, continually spinning it round and round in a
> most ludicrous fashion; and when we came to some jungle
> he added to the absurdity of his appearance by taking off
> his only article of clothing—his loincloth . . . the sight of a
> perfectly naked negro walking under an umbrella was too
> much for my gravity, and I fairly exploded with laughter.

In this example, the umbrella is an object highly valued by both
parties, but the Englishman cannot divorce it from its context, in his
own culture, of certain codes of dress and presentation, leading him to
find only absurdity in the African man's pride and satisfaction.

A fascinating example of the colonial brolly may be found in
Georges Méliès's *Le Voyage dans la Lune* (*A Trip to the Moon*). This
1902 silent film follows a disordered gaggle of umbrella-toting astronomers as they travel to the moon and back in a capsule fired
from a cannon. On the surface of the moon, they encounter a group
of moon people (or Selenites) and promptly proceed to attack them
with their umbrellas. A couple of blows, it turns out, are sufficient
to dispatch each Selenite in a cloud of smoke.[13] Following these un-
provoked attacks, the astronomers proceed to murder the Selenites'
king and take another Selenite captive, tying it up and exhibiting
it to the public on their return to Earth—"a pointed commentary,"
film scholar Matthew Solomon observes, "on the unfortunate consequences of colonialism."

---

13 A far more peaceable use for the umbrellas may be observed earlier in the same scene,
when it is discovered that planting an umbrella on the moon causes it to grow into a
giant mushroom.

Ariel Beaujot's research into umbrella narratives across the rapidly proliferating printed media of the Victorian period suggests that, back on British soil, umbrella use was not merely a fashion choice; it also reflected widespread themes of imperialism, democracy and race operating at the time.

The British were robustly proud of their democracy and considered nondemocratic countries to be substantially less civilized than their own. Beaujot draws an intriguing parallel between the governance of these respective regions and their policies of umbrella use: while umbrellas were democratically available in Britain (to anyone, that is, who could afford to purchase one), umbrella use in most nondemocratic countries operated under similar, nondemocratic hierarchies as those observed in India and China. This tension between "democratic versus despotic" governance and umbrella use often played out across the glut of umbrella stories and essays published in magazines of the time.

Beaujot's research shows that Victorian purveyors of brolly history downplayed the umbrella's links with Asia, Africa and other colonized countries, and instead emphasized its Greek history—despite the fact that, in Beaujot's opinion, the British umbrella owed far less to Greece than it did to Asia. However—especially in a period when Greco-Roman history was informing Enlightenment art, architecture, culture and philosophy—it suited the Victorians far better to credit the birthplace of democracy with inventing umbrellas, instead of the countries they were busy enforcing political, cultural and moral supremacy over. Similarly, writers and umbrella historians alike played up stories of unusual (to the English) umbrella customs and umbrella-related superstitions in parts of Asia and Africa in order to enhance the sense, as Beaujot puts it, "that Britain should exert a civilizing influence over them." One of these so-called unusual customs was using the umbrella as the very thing it was originally designed for: a sunshade. The English assumed a sense of moral superiority for "discovering" the usefulness of umbrellas in the rain. This superiority came through in their umbrella narratives; as Beaujot observes, "Underlying many of the stories of the non-Western history of the umbrella was a feeling that people who used it only for the sun were odd and in need of education."

As if this pervasive whitewashing of the umbrella's rich cultural history wasn't pernicious enough, Beaujot suggests that even parasol use amongst Victorian British women had imperial overtones. At the time the skin tone of British women (specifically *women*) "was carefully constructed as a way to emphasize racial difference . . . [w]omen were encouraged to maintain their skin as white, which was the standard skin colour that all other races were measured against." By using parasols, middle- and upper-class women were able to protect their skin from sun damage and preserve the Victorian ideal of whiteness. Thus, Beaujot argues, Britons were "actively maintaining their status as a white race *through middle-class women* [italics mine]"—and, in doing so, exaggeratedly performing the very rituals of parasol use they derided in the colonized.

The oppressors, however, should not have been so smug. In staking their claims to culturally superior umbrella use, they were in fact willfully ignoring their own history. As it happens, the good British citizens of pre-Victorian times did not look kindly upon the umbrella at all. Where the Victorian brolly served as an indicator of social and imperial standing, its eighteenth-century predecessor was positively scorned, and all who dared to carry one faced ridicule and abuse in the streets.

2 ‖ DISREPUTABLE OBJECTS

IN HER ILLUMINATING book *Rain: A Natural and Cultural History* (2015), Cynthia Barnett devotes an entire chapter to the "great articles of rain": mackintoshes, windscreen wipers and umbrellas. Besides their obvious functions of deflecting rainwater from body or glass, these objects all have one curious thing in common. Each of these inventions—now so seamlessly integrated into our everyday lives that it is easy to forget they were ever "invented" at all—was initially met with ridicule of the highest order.

When Jonas Hanway (1712–1786)—businessman, philanthropist and social campaigner—returned to England from travels through Russia and the Middle East, he brought with him many treasures and curiosities, amongst them some revolutionary ideas about the potential of umbrellas. He had no doubt observed them employed as sun protection in Persia, and back at home found them rather useful for protecting one's clothing and wig from the rain. He was, however, quite singular in his preferences. The majority of Londoners were baffled—even affronted—by his enthusiasm for

OPPOSITE: Jonas Hanway, stubbornly impervious to curious stares, outright impertinence—and rainwater

brollies. Despite the curious stares, bewilderment and heckling he met with on the streets, Hanway persisted with his umbrella until the end of his life. It was only after his death that his good sense caught on with the general populace.

In France, umbrella and parasol production began in earnest in the early 1700s, but Britain would not catch up for at least half a century. A French visitor to London noted, in 1772, that "it is a rule with the people of London not to use, or suffer foreigners to use, our umbrellas of taffeta or waxed silk." Exactly how the good humans of London enforced this policy is not specified.

But even in France umbrellas could be looked upon with disfavour. As Octave Uzanne reflected in his 1883 book *The Sunshade, the Glove, the Muff,* "the dandyism of 1830, which pretended that the carrying of a walking-stick required a particular skill, repelled the umbrella as contrary to veritable elegance. The umbrella was countrified, the property of gaffer and gammer; it was tolerable only in the hands of anyone who had long renounced all pretensions to any charm." Honoré de Balzac reputedly described the object as "a bastard born of the walking-stick and the cabriolet."[14] In 1768, commenting on Paris fashion, the Marquis Caraccioli wrote:

> For some time now, it has been the custom never to go out without an umbrella and to submit to the inconvenience of carrying it under the arm for six months in order to use it, at a generous computation, possibly six times. Those, however, who do not wish to be taken as belonging to the vulgar herd, prefer to risk a wetting.

It would take some time for such a "vulgar herd" to aggregate on British soil, as this anecdote makes abundantly clear: in the early

---

14 Crawford, amongst others, attributes this to *A Treatise on Elegant Living* (1830), although I found no trace of it in a recent reading.

1780s a Dr John Jamieson, carrying a large yellow Parisian umbrella through Glasgow, created such a stir that crowds actually began *following* him down the streets.

After Hanway's stubborn yet pioneering use, clergymen became one of the first groups to take up umbrellas, possibly because of their familiarity with older, larger models often used to protect mourners in churchyards, and possibly because, in Crawford's opinion, "their cloth guaranteed immunity from offensive criticism."

Did it, though? This excerpt from Hilary Mantel's novel *The Giant, O'Brien* (1998), set in 1780s London, paints a slightly different picture:

> At nine-thirty that evening it was still light, but it had begun to drizzle. Bitch Mary, crouching by the window, made a squeak of surprise; they all swarmed—except the Giant—to see what it was, and within seconds Claffey, Pybus and Jankin were down the stairs and out.
>
> "What was it?" said the Giant . . .
>
> "It was an Englishman," Bitch Mary said. "Walking beneath a canopy on a stick."
>
> "Umbrella," Joe said, bored. "The apprentices are always turning out against them. It's a fact that they are easy prey because carried by their clergymen and the more fussy and nervous type of old fellow . . . The boys like to throw stones after, then chase the fellows and collapse the tent on their heads, making them sopping."

Several writers have expressed surprise at the length of time it took the British—residents (anecdotally, if not entirely factually) of one of the most persistently gloomy islands on the planet—to acf cept umbrellas as an item of everyday equipage. William Sangster (umbrella-maker) wondered "[w]hy so much unmerited ridicule should be poured upon the head (or handle) of the devoted

Umbrella . . . What is there comic in an Umbrella?" One hundred and sixty years later, Cynthia Barnett considers it "hard to believe that people once spurned umbrellas . . . It was as if," she muses, "God didn't want them to spurn His heaven-sent creation."

This spiritual argument has some truth to it. Londoners did criticize Hanway "for defying the heavenly purpose of rain, which obviously was to make people wet," according to Crawford. But there was also a more corporeal element. Bitch Mary from *The Giant, O'Brien* sneers at umbrella-carriers, those "who think rain will run through their skins and dilute their blood." Those who carried them were "old fogies, careful of their health," in Sangster's words; in Stevenson's, it was "the hypochrondriacal, out of solicitude for their health, or the frugal, out of care for their raiment."

Coachmen felt threatened by the umbrella: if every pedestrian were to carry one, what would happen to their livelihood?[15] Meanwhile, the (ever-critical) Marquis Caraccioli sneered at umbrella use as "a sure sign that one possesses no carriage." In his memoir of 1770, an English footman named John MacDonald recorded the harassment he received on the streets for daring to carry a silk umbrella: "Frenchman, why do you not get a coach, Monsieur?" After nearly two thousand years of using capes, oiled cloaks and mantles for protection against the rain, this new-fangled contraption was viewed with something approaching disbelief. Who did people think they were, to defy the very skies? To parade their frugality on the streets? Or, to take a slightly different view of it, to pretend to a luxury—sheltered transport—only available to the wealthy?

It is a rare object that can transcend the human meaning invested in it, and the umbrella was not one of them. For a long time its only socially acceptable uses were for getting from building to

---

15 This, as Sangster notes, was an interesting reversal of the protests made by watermen when hackney coaches were first introduced: those who made their living ferrying people across the Thames were of the opinion that people "should travel by river, not by road."

carriage and back again on rainy days, or for planting in the churchyard to shelter mourners at funerals. Women carried umbrellas often enough for men to be deterred by the threat of appearing effeminate (more on that later).

People's resistance to new ideas extended beyond umbrellas (and mackintoshes and, when the time came, windscreen wipers). As Lou Carver reports in *Victoriana Magazine*, when John Hetherington donned one of the nation's first top hats in 1797, the reaction on the street was so extreme that the unfortunate gentleman was arrested and charged with wearing "a tall structure having a shining luster calculated to frighten timid people." His hat had attracted such a crowd that women fainted, children screamed, dogs howled and an errand boy fell and broke his arm. Yet forty years later, no gentleman would be seen without one.

The reception, in the nineteenth century, of early attempts at weather forecasting was similar but far more sobering. As Cynthia Barnett relates, when naval captain Robert FitzRoy—who famously commanded the HMS *Beagle* on its voyage with Charles Darwin—was chosen to establish Britain's first weather bureau, Britain was not quite ready. His pioneering work—using weather data like rainfall and barometric readings to predict future weather patterns and limit disasters like the Royal Charter Storm of 1859 (in which nearly two hundred ships and over eight hundred sailors were lost to the deeps)—was met with fierce derision and, after a few years, FitzRoy took a razor to his throat. There were doubtless many factors contributing to his death, not least FitzRoy's ongoing struggles with depression, but his suicide confirmed the public in their opinions that "forecasting" (a term FitzRoy had coined) was, in Barnett's words, "an immoral pseudo-science," and England banned forecasting acgtivities for the next thirteen years.[16]

---

16 Happily, skepticism did not run so high in America: Barnett reports that in 1870 meteorological duties were assigned to the office of the secretary of war.

Next to this, an antipathy towards umbrellas seems positively cute.

However, the antipathy stuck, and for some time the umbrella was linked with ideas of shabbiness, dishevelment and limited means—in short, with the lower classes. Jonathan Swift's 1710 poem "Description of a City Shower" places the umbrella firmly in the hands of a working-class woman, while her wealthy counterparts take shelter in shops:

> *Now in contiguous drops the flood comes down,*
> *Threat'ning with deluge this devoted town:*
> *To shops in crowds the dragged females fly,*
> *Pretend to cheapen goods, but nothing buy.*
> *The Templar spruce, while every spout's abroach,*
> *Stays till 'tis fair, yet seems to call a coach.*
> *The tuck'd up sempstress walks with hasty strides*
> *While streams run down her oil'd umbrella's sides.*

None are more eloquent on the subject of brollies than Charles Dickens. Dickens's work is richly populated with umbrellas and umbrella-wielders. In *The Violent Effigy: A Study of Dickens' Imagination* (1973), literary critic John Carey expounds on their role as social indicators: "Elaborately undignified, they immediately locate their owner in the lower class." Sarah Gamp, the nurse in Dickens's *Martin Chuzzlewit* (serialized from 1843 to 1844), is, although only a minor character in the story, arguably one of the best known. Her extraordinary brand of nursing—an admixture of sloth, greed, drunkenness and extravagant self-admiration—is underscored throughout by her ever-present umbrella: "a species of gig umbrella; the latter article in colour like a faded leaf, except where a circular patch of lively blue had been dexterously let in at the top." Like Mrs Gamp herself, this umbrella is not known for its subtlety:

> The umbrella . . . was particularly hard to be got rid of, and several times thrust out its battered brass nozzle from

improper crevices and chinks, to the great terror of the other passengers. Indeed, in her intense anxiety to find a haven of refuge for this chattel, Mrs Gamp so often moved it, in the course of five minutes, that it seemed not one umbrella but fifty.

In fact, one begins to suspect it of having designs on the good health of those nearby:

Tom, with Ruth upon his arm, stood looking down from the wharf, as nearly regardless as it was in the nature of flesh and blood to be, of an elderly lady behind him, who had brought a large umbrella with her, and didn't know what to do with it. This tremendous instrument had a hooked handle; and its vicinity was first made known to him by a painful pressure on the windpipe, consequent upon its having caught him round the throat. Soon after disengaging himself with perfect good humour, he had a sensation of the ferule in his back; immediately afterwards, of the hook entangling his ankles; then of the umbrella generally, wandering about his hat, and flapping at it like a great bird; and, lastly, of a poke or thrust below the ribs, which gave him such exceeding anguish, that he could not refrain from turning around to offer a mild remonstrance.

It didn't take long for "gamp" to enter the vernacular, not only as a byword for "umbrella" but for "nurse" as well: "two things," as John Bowen notes in "Dickens's Umbrellas," "admitted to the bourgeois home that are meant to protect you from harm but which may in fact have the opposite effect. Like Robinson Crusoe, Mrs Gamp leapt off of the page and into the vocabulary of the day.

Elsewhere in the novel, Martin Chuzzlewit and his friend Mark Tapley travel through America in search of land on which to speculate. They meet a man called General Choke, who cons

Gamp sports gamp

them into settling their funds on a disastrous piece of land. An umbrella gives readers a comically obvious clue to the character of the man who uses it.

> "Here am I, sir," said the General, setting up his umbrella
> to represent himself; and a villainous-looking umbrella
> it was; a very bad counter to stand for the sterling coin of
> his benevolence; "here am I with my grey hairs, sir, and

a moral sense. Would I, with my principles, invest capital
in this speculation if I didn't think it full of hopes and
chances for my brother man?"

Over the coming months, hopes and chances give way to disease
and despair, and Martin and Mark are lucky to escape with their
lives. If only they had heeded that brolly.

A fascinating real-world example of a disruptive, disreputable brolly may be found in the figure of Theodora Grahn, a late-
eighteenth-century and almost undoubtedly transgender person
who lived and dressed as a man. Theodora—the self-styled Baron
de Verdion (1744–1802)—possessed an almost unquenchable apa
petite for both eating and drinking, and was described in *Kirby's
Wonderful and Scientific Museum, or, Magazine of Remarkable
Characters* (a telling title in itself) as

> extremely grotesque: from her large cocked hat and
> bagged hair, with her boots, cane and umbrella, which
> she carried in all weathers. The latter of which she invari-
> ably carried in her hand, resting upon her back.

As if the description weren't censorious enough, the brief biog-
raphy from which it is drawn tells of a lifetime of struggles against
men determined to reveal the baron's "true" female sex: one attack
was humiliating enough to drive Verdion to resettle in London from
his native Berlin. As Crawford points out, in a period when umbrellas were more or less maligned, their ready association with such
a radical (for the time) individual could hardly have improved the
umbrella's reputation in conservative British social circles.[17]

---

17 *Kirby's Wonderful and Scientific Museum, or, Magazine of Remarkable Characters*,
vol. 2, is available free online. The entry about the Baron de Verdion covers several
pages, and makes for fascinating reading.

Deep-seated and pervasive though it was, disdain for the umbrella didn't just come down to social mores, or British people being "stuck in the muck of custom," as Cynthia Barnett puts it. Indeed, two tangible factors needed to change before the umbrella could find widespread acceptance.

The first was the state of the streets. In one particularly enlightening passage in Sangster's book, Mr Pugh, biographer of Jonas Hanway, describes what it was like to walk the streets of London before they were universally paved.[18] "It is not easy to convey to a person," he writes, "a tolerable idea of their inconvenience and uncleanliness." He describes a multitude of shop signs extending from the buildings into the street, staggered so they would not meet, and greatly impeding sight lines. Some footpaths were so narrow they would admit only one person at a time, and even then they were partially blocked by a row of posts running edge-wise along the carriage way:

> He whose urgent business would not permit of his keeping pace with the gentleman of leisure before him, turned out between the two posts . . . into the carriage-way. When he perceived danger moving toward him, he wished to return within the protection of the row of posts; but there was commonly a rail continued from the top of one post to that of another . . . in which case he was obliged to run back to the first inlet, or climb over, or creep under the railing, in attempting which, he might be fortunate if he escaped with no other injury than what proceeded from dirt.

---

18 The following passages are reproduced almost verbatim (and without credit) in American umbrella manufacturers Clyde and Black's *Umbrellas and Their History* (1864)—except that New York is substituted for London!

If he were too intimidated by the dangers of walking in the carriage way, he was obliged to displace anyone on the footpath in front of him, which, when met with resistance, "made his journey truly a warfare." Pugh elaborates on the discomforts presented to an "unfortunate female, stopped in the street on a windy day under a large old sign loaded with lead and iron in full swing over her head . . . and perhaps a torrent of rain and dirty water falling near from a projecting spout." Add to these various obstructions—above and to either side—the fact that hooped skirts were then in fashion, and it's no small wonder that people were reluctant to add umbrellas to the mix.

However, the second, and very best, explanation for early umbrella disparagement lies with the objects themselves. Dickens may gently mock when he describes, in Mrs Gamp's flat, her umbrella, "which as something of great price and rarity, was displayed with particular ostentation"—but at the time, the cost of such articles was significant and not remotely commensurate with their quality or usefulness. Before Mr Fox pioneered the steel frame, umbrellas were made with whalebone, and they were heavy, labour-intensive affairs. The ribs were not hinged at the stick but strung on a wire, and apt to become disordered. The whalebone was liable to crack if not dried with the utmost care. Coats of wax or oil waterproofing were not sufficient to keep the huge cotton covers from soaking through, and once the umbrella was folded up again it had to be carried under the arm, wetting one. The whole structure more closely resembled a loosely ordered bundle of twigs swaddled in heavy fabric than it did the modern-day brolly.

Such unwieldy objects, when adopted, necessarily presented their bearers with certain difficulties in negotiating crowded streets and inclement weather. In 1801, J. S. Duncan produced a popular little pamphlet entitled *Hints to the Bearers of Walking Sticks and Umbrellas*, in which he satirized the worst types of umbrella behaviour on the streets. Some of the caricatures are still recognizable today, but when you factor in the struggles of keeping an early umbrella elevated, and its bone work in order, along with the heavy flappy wetness of the thing, you get some idea of the obstacles faced by umbrella pioneers (and their fellow citizenry).

Duncan sorted the kingdom of umbrella-carriers into several different phyla: the Shield-Bearer (he who "drives his Umbrella before him, covering completely his head and body"); the Sky-Striker (who, in passing other umbrella-bearers, "jerks up his umbrella to the sky, whereby the shorter endangers with the points of his whalebone the eyes of the taller"); the Mud-Scooper (who, in passing other umbrella-bearers, "dashes it to the ground so as to impede all passage"; and the Inverters ("those careless beings who present the inside of the Umbrella to the wind, whereby the cover is turned inside out, and commonly much lacerated, while they impede the progress of many a time-pressed citizen, during the awkward attempts to re-arrange it").

Others presented less danger to passersby than to themselves:

> The Self-Tormentor . . . is usually the principal sufferer by his own negligence. Poor Spinbrain . . . spread his umbrella, and set out for Leadenhall-street, amidst a heavy shower of rain. He could not refrain from gazing at a printshop window, regardless of a cataract that fell from a spout above his head. He sloped his Umbrella, so that the cover pressed closely on his back, and conveyed the flood into his pocket.

Here, Duncan lays the blame on the bearer, rather than the object itself. The two leading ladies of Sarah Perry's novel *The Essex Serpent* (2016)—set in late-nineteenth-century England—may beg to differ: on a walk through Colchester their umbrella "had done nothing more than channel the weak rain more efficiently into the collars of their coats."

A Sky-Striker and a Shield-Bearer battle it out

The umbrella has indeed come a long way. In 1855 alone, over three hundred patents were submitted for improvements to the umbrella's design and manufacture. Add to those patents the vast improvements made to materials and technologies since 1855 and you have the brolly today: 100 percent waterproof, lightweight and stashable in all but the daintiest of handbags.

Possibly the most infamous illustration of the fluctuating role that umbrellas have occupied in the public imagination comes from twentieth-century Britain. Neville Chamberlain, British prime minister from 1937 to 1940, experienced a surge of popularity followed

Inverters 5

y striker   A Mud-Scooper

by a spectacular fall from grace in the tumultuous lead-up to World War II—and as a conspicuous public brolly-bearer, so too did his umbrella. The umbrella in question—a distinguished black specq imen from Thomas Brigg & Sons, forebear of the Swaine Adeney Brigg umbrella shop, still trading in the heart of London—was, like Thatcher's handbag and Churchill's cigar, Chamberlain's signal prop. As historian Professor Sir David Cannadine explains in his broadcast "Neville Chamberlain's Umbrella,"[19] the umbrella came to represent everything Chamberlain stood for in the uncertain atmosphere of prewar Britain:

> To his supporters, Neville Chamberlain was as trustworthy and reliable as his brolly, and his policy of appeasing the dictators, which he pursued so single-mindedly during the late 1930s, was the only way to preserve peace, and to keep the German bombs from raining down on British cities.

Cannadine describes Chamberlain as, like his umbrella, "austere, uptight, and tightly furled," but these dubious attributes didn't curtail the waves of public adoration that broke out when Chamberlain signed the Munich Agreement, supposedly averting war. Chamberlain was showered with gifts (including, unsurprisingly, a fair few umbrellas), and umbrella sales dramatically increased in England, America, India and across Europe. Umbrellas took hold of the public imagination: sugar umbrellas were displayed in shop windows across London, while in Paris a new dance emerged where participants hooked their chosen partners with the handle of an umbrella. For a time, umbrellas were known as "Chamberlains."

---

19 To which much of the following information must be credited—and if you have a spare fifteen minutes, the programme itself is well worth a listen.

PRECEDING PAGES: Inverters fight the wind while a Mud-Scooper trips a careless Sky-Striker.

A popular joke at the time held that Chamberlain should write a response to Hitler's *Mein Kampf* and title it *Mein Gamp*. A cocktail named "The Umbrella" was even invented in Chamberlain's honour. In Cannadine's words,

> Chamberlain's umbrella had been miraculously transformed into an olive branch, which had proved mightier than the sword, and it became the symbol of that triumph.

This period of umbrella-related adulations was, inevitably, all too brief. Soon, the political climate took a turn for the worse, the Munich Agreement was thrown to the wind and Europe descended into war. Chamberlain similarly descended—from the heights of popularity to the depths of public scorn—and with him went his umbrella. Hitler had looked upon Chamberlain as "that silly old man with his umbrella," mocking what he described as the "umbrella pacifism" of the once-great British Empire, and the reaction of the British public followed suit. Cannadine continues:

> Instead of being an admired emblem of decency, honesty and good will, Chamberlain's brolly was now ridiculed, as an indication of his prim, provincial and naïve gullibility. Where once his umbrella had embodied high-minded strength, it was now associated with self-righteous weakness.

And as if all that weren't enough, Hitler named the 1940 bombing campaign of Birmingham—Chamberlain's hometown—*Regenschirm*, or, "umbrella."

In just a few short months, Neville Chamberlain's umbrella went from revered to reviled. Perhaps no other umbrella has experienced such a shocking transformation. However, transformation or no, disreputable brollies continue to haunt the pages of writing today.

Whether it's a shabby object in the hands of a half-giant, the signal prop of a woman shunned by society or the catalyst for an explosive interaction between two fairly repugnant middle-class characters, the umbrella remains intertwined with class, social stigma and human decency.

In Emma Healey's bestselling 2014 novel *Elizabeth Is Missing*, the central character, Maud, reflects on the "mad woman" who once lived in her neighbourhood. The woman is characterized by, above all things, her umbrella:

> She always carried an umbrella, a shabby inky thing, half unfurled in a way that made it look like an injured bird. She used to stop the buses by standing in front of them and waving the umbrella, and then she would lift her dress and show her knickers. They said it was because her daughter had been knocked down and killed by a bus, before the war. People talked about it in whispers, or they made sly jokes, but if you asked a question you'd be told to be quiet, not to pry, just to keep away from her, as if she had something catching.

The woman scares Maud: she attacks Maud with her umbrella, chases her in the street and tries to communicate cryptic messages without speech. When the woman is hit by a car in front of the young Maud's house she suddenly seems less frightening, "crumpled up and tiny," partly because she has been disarmed: "She didn't even have her umbrella." Her umbrella is so closely associated with her unsettling nature that, when it turns up in another character's room, its mere presence disturbs Maud enough to suspect him of murder. Madness, motherhood and umbrellas are also linked in Ruth Park's *The Harp in the South* (1948), in the form of "Aunt Kathy, her that had eight children and a pillar of the Church for a husband, and then went mad and danced Salome's dance in her skin and an umbrella."

Harry Potter and the Philosopher's Stone (1997), by J. K. Rowling, contains a spectacularly disruptive brolly. Harry's uncle Vernon Dursley is the director of a company, comfortably middle class, and "perfectly normal, thank you very much." He and his wife Petunia live on a neat, pristine street, send their son Dudley to a private boys' school and shower him with expensive gifts. Their nephew Harry, with his "all stubbornly messy" hair and ungovernable talent for making odd things happen, is the one thorn in their perfect, ordered existence.

From the very first, the *Harry Potter* series portrays magic as a disturbance in the order of things. "Drifts of owls stream through the sky in broad daylight, people wearing long colourful robes gather in excited huddles on the street and showers of shooting stars light up the night sky." The story unfolds to reveal a wizarding world richly peopled with a cast of scruffy, eccentric characters, a drama set in motion when, in the early hours of Harry's eleventh birthday, a hulking half giant named Hagrid bursts into the room and threatens Vernon Dursley with a dilapidated umbrella:

> "Now you listen here, boy," [Uncle Vernon] snarled, "I accept there's something strange about you, probably nothing a good beating wouldn't have cured . . . as for . . . your parents, well, they were weirdos, no denying it . . . the world's better off without them . . . "
>
> Hagrid leapt from the sofa and drew a battered pink umbrella from inside his coat. Pointing this at Uncle Vernon like a sword, he said, "I'm warning you, Dursley . . . one more word . . . "
>
> In danger of being speared on the end of an umbrella by a bearded giant, Uncle Vernon's courage failed again; he flattened himself against the wall and fell silent.

On an associated note, the troll-leg umbrella-stand in the hall-way of Number 12, Grimmauld Place, introduced in *Harry Potter and the Order of the Phoenix* (2003), functions as a grisly reminder of the deadly prejudice amongst some in the wizarding world against magical creatures and muggles (nonmagical humans).

An ugly little scene unfolds around an umbrella in Hanif Kureishi's short story "The Umbrella" (1999). In it, an estranged husband and wife bicker when he returns their two sons to her house on a rainy day. He asks for the loan of an umbrella, and just as she has refused to grant him a divorce, she refuses to give him an umbrella; incensed, he forces his way into the house ("She did bang her head, but it was, in football jargon, a 'dive.'") and seizes one from the closet. She then proceeds to punch him. Of course, the story is not about an umbrella at all, but rather the man's "deep, intellectual and emotional hatred" towards his wife and his desire to "pulverize" her, for which the umbrella acts as a lightning rod. Disreputable object indeed.

William Sangster's indignation about the historical abuses of the English umbrella remains, so many years later, palpable. The umbrella, he insists, was treated in "a most ungrateful . . . fashion" and with "shameful neglect." In *Bring Me Sunshine* (2012), a book about the charming vagaries of British weather, Charlie Connelly echoes the sentiment: "They perform an entirely selfless function and how do we treat them? We leave them on buses, on trains, in pubs." Listening to them both, you could be forgiven for thinking that umbrellas were sentient. And in some respects, they very nearly were, for umbrellas have possessed layers of meaning far more mystical than merely signaling the status of monarchs, slave traders and Great Moguls, or the lowered rank of their subjects.

Mr Tumnus and Lucy, or, the first act of umbrella-ing

3 ‖ SHELTER, SHADOW, SHIELD

S O FAR WE have seen the umbrella encompass a range of social meanings, all related to sovereignty, rank, class, income
or nationality. These meanings are anchored in the objects themselves, from the handles (parrot headed, "hooky" or "nobbly") to
the canopies (decked in jewels, broad and white or "all gone along
the seams") to the very ferrules (battered nozzles and probing tips).
However, there is another layer of meaning that derives less from the
physical object than from its function—which is, of course, protection. Umbrellas are shields interposed between the bearer and the
sky: they create shelter within their shadows.

The central character of José Eduardo Agualusa's *A General
Theory of Oblivion* (2012) understands this all too well. Gripped
with a fear of open spaces, Ludovica finds relief in an umbrella interposed between herself and the heavens:

> Ludovica never liked having to face the sky. While still
> only a little girl, she was horrified by open spaces. She
> felt, upon leaving the house, fragile and vulnerable, like a
> turtle whose shell had been torn off. When she was very

small—six, seven years old—she was already refusing to go to school without the protection of a vast black umbrella, whatever the weather.

The extremity of her need for shelter is highlighted when, years later, she finds the umbrella too cumbersome for gardening and swaps this commonplace solution for something rather more comic:

> In the first months of her isolation, Ludo only rarely went without the security of her umbrella when she visited the terrace. Later, she began using a long cardboard box, in which she had cut two holes at eye level for looking through, and two others to the sides, lower down, to keep her arms free . . . anybody looking at the building from another of similar height would see a large box moving around, leaning out and drawing itself back in again.

All of which brings us to an important side note on the parasol. Umbrella scholars (not all of them Victorian imperialists) and fashionable societies throughout history have often been at pains to distinguish between the two (particularly where gender is concerned, as we will see later)—a curious approach, given that all umbrellas, as we have seen, are descended from the parasol. While they certainly have their differences—and sometimes the most well-intentioned parasol simply *won't* keep the rain off—the fact remains that all obF jects conforming to this basic shape and structure do keep *something* off, and whatever is kept off is of less significance than the act of sheltering, shadowing and shielding that these objects provide.

That said, there is one very important, yet blindingly obvious, meaning attached to the umbrella that we have, thus far, sidelined, and that is: rain. Nothing quite signifies rain like an umbrella. The sentence "Pack an umbrella" is commensurate with "It's probably going to rain." An umbrella symbol inked on a box is universally understood to mean: do not get this box wet. It's a neat twist of logic

(Do not get this book wet)

that an object intended to maintain dryness has come to signify conditions of wetness.

The lovable and eponymous bear of A. A. Milne's *Winnie-the-Pooh* (1926) relies on this selfsame twist of logic in the story "In Which We Are Introduced to Winnie-the-Pooh and Some Bees, and the Stories Begin." When Pooh spots a beehive high in a tree, he comes up with a daring plan to replenish the honey pots in his larder: he will roll in some mud and float up to the hive beneath a blue balloon, pretending to be a little black cloud hovering beneath a scrap of sky. His cunning deception, however, does not appear to work on the bees:

> "Christopher Robin!" [Pooh] said in a loud whisper.
> "Hallo!"
> "I think the bees *suspect* something!"
> "What sort of thing?"
> "I don't know. But something tells me that they're suspicious!"
> "Perhaps they think that you're after their honey?"

"It may be that. You never can tell with bees." There was another little silence, and then he called down to you again.

"Christopher Robin!"

"Yes?"

"Have you an umbrella in your house?"

"I think so."

"I wish you would bring it out here, and walk up and down with it, and look up at me every now and then, and say "Tut-tut, it looks like rain." I think, if you did that, it would help the deception which we are practicing on these bees."

It is this same cultural understanding that Captain Wentworth riffs on in Jane Austen's *Persuasion* (1817), with a little joke at the expense of the English city he is visiting:

Captain Wentworth . . . turned again to Anne, and by manner, rather than words, was offering his services to her.

"I am much obliged to you," was her answer, "but . . . [the] carriage would not accommodate so many. I walk. I prefer walking."

"But it rains."

"Oh! very little. Nothing that I regard."

After a moment's pause he said, "Though I came only yesterday, I have equipped myself properly for Bath already, you see," (pointing to a new umbrella) "I wish you would make use of it, if you are determined to walk."

In fact, when treated with a healthy dose of Murphy's law, this same understanding is the very reason my venerable grandfather called his umbrella "the drought stick": for whenever you carry it around in expectation of rain, it will not do so. He is not the only one to have made this observation; Robert Louis Stevenson noted the same phenomenon back in 1894:

> Not the least important, and by far the most curious property of the umbrella, is the energy which it displays in affecting the atmospheric strata. There is no fact in meteorology better established—indeed, it is almost the only one on which meteorologists are agreed—than that the carriage of an umbrella produces desiccation of the air; while if it be left at home, aqueous vapour is largely produced, and is soon deposited in the form of rain.

One fascinating aspect of the history of British umbrella use is that the word and its meaning seem to have vastly predated use of the object itself. Crawford dates the "earliest noted contextual use of the word 'umbrella'" to 1609, in a letter from John Donne to Sir Henry Goodyer:

> We are so composed that if abundance or glory scorch and melt us, we have an earthly cave, our bodies, to go into by consideration and cool ourselves, and if we be frozen, and contracted with lower and dark fortunes, we have within us a torch, a soul, lighter and warmer than any without; we are therefore our own umbrella and our own suns.

In this, as in other early references, Crawford observes that the word "umbrella" functions as "a commonly used metaphor for any form of shelter or protection." Even today it serves this purpose, for beyond its literal meaning, the *Oxford English Dictionary* defines it variously as:

2   **a.** a means of shelter or protection.
     b. a screen, a disguise.

6   **b.** acting as an overall coordinating or unifying agency;
     covering or protecting a number of things; (of a word,
     name etc.) covering a number of meanings or con-
     cepts; general, catch-all.

And in the past participle:

> **umbrellaed:** protected or covered *as by an umbrella*; pro-
> vided with an umbrella or umbrellas . . . [italics mine]

The associations of shelter and protection are as ancient as umbrellas themselves, and feed into the profound religious and mytho-
logical meaning once invested in the objects.

One of the oldest deities in ancient Egypt was Nut, goddess of
the sky. She didn't just represent the sky: she *was* the sky, stretched
across the Earth from toes to fingertips in an immense dome shape,
her body strewn with stars. Her brother, Geb, was god of the Earth.
It was the job of their father, Shu, to ensure they never met, and he
supported Nut with one hand on her breast and the other on her
thigh. Together, as Crawford points out, they resemble an enormous,
cosmological umbrella, and their pairing was often depicted on
sarcophagi.

Thus, when umbrellas were used to shield the monarchs of ancient Egypt, they weren't only providing sun protection: they also
signified the vault of heaven stretching over the king, denoting his
divine stature. And the "shade" below the king's umbrella was also
symbolic. There is some disagreement amongst umbrella scholars
as to what exactly the symbolism meant: according to Crawford the
umbrella's shadow represented the protection of the king; Beaujot's
research, however, suggests that it represented the king's power over
not only his people but over the sun itself. By simply casting the

Nut, Geb and Shu: brolliological cosmology

shadow of his umbrella over others, he could enslave or kill those around him. Either way—whether comforting or ruthless, protecting or condemning—the umbrella was certainly a profound symbolic manifestation of the king's power. In India, the Sanskrit writer Kālidāsa wrote a play called *The Recognition of Śakuntalā*, in which King Dushyanta describes how

> the cares of supporting the nation harass the sovereign,
> while he is cheered with a view of the people's welfare,
> as a huge umbrella, of which a man bears the staff in his
> own hand, fatigues while it shades him. The sovereign,
> like a branching tree, bears on his head the scorching
> sunbeams, while the broad shade allays the fever of those
> who seek shelter under him.

Even today, a canopy is held over English monarchs during anointment, the most sacred part of the coronation ceremony—a practice that Crawford directly links back to ancient Egyptian beliefs connecting canopies, kingship and divinity. Indeed, the umbrella has played its part in Christianity as well: by the eighth century B.C.E. it was associated with the Catholic Church, and during the Middle Ages it was traditionally held over the pope in processions. Papal insignia of the fifteenth century consisted of an umbrella and crossed keys.

In China, the umbrella also possessed cosmic significance. According to Confucian texts, chariot parasols acted as depictions of the universe itself: the stick represented the axis of the universe, while the twenty-eight radiating ribs signified the stars. Thus, the parasol signified a Zhou king's omnipotence in the very act of sheltering him.

Umbrellas are also closely identified with Buddhist traditions. The umbrella is listed as one of the Buddha's Eight Auspicious Symbols and is therefore considered lucky—in fact, artistic depictions of the Buddha occasionally include umbrellas. Similarly, in early Buddhist carvings an umbrella over an empty space signified the invisible presence of Buddha—not dissimilar to the light that burns before the tabernacle, indicating the Christian god's unswerving presence. Umbrellas and Buddhism were so closely linked that the spread of the religion from India to China and Southeast Asia cemented popular associations between umbrellas and spiritual significance long before European contact. One of the Jātaka tales (a body of Indian literature chronicling the various births of Buddha) describes the god Brahma holding a white umbrella over Buddha's head after his birth. Tibetan temples were hung with large silk parasols, or *gdugs*, above their altars, and the goddess Sitātapatrā—Sanskrit for "White Parasol"—is a protector against evil and black magic in the Mahayana and Vajrayana traditions.

The shelter of an umbrella has been linked with the protection of gods and kings since ancient times. Thus, inviting someone to share an umbrella is more than just an act of kindness: it bears a wealth of religious and historical associations, and lends an added poignancy to a number of literary examples.

In E. M. Forster's *A Room with a View* (1908), Lucy Honeychurch's Italian holiday takes an unexpected turn when she is kissed in a field of violets by a man she is neither promised nor married to. Her sanctimonious cousin Charlotte Bartlett witnesses the encounter and immediately undertakes to save Lucy from the disastrous situation. Lucy's feelings for the man might have moved her to object, but her cousin's swift intervention and her reassuring presence under a shared parasol in a sudden storm leave her powerless:

> Rain and darkness came on together. The two ladies huddled together under an inadequate parasol. There was a lightning flash, and Miss Lavish, who was nervous, screamed from the carriage in front. At the next flash, Lucy screamed also . . . Under the rug, Lucy felt the kindly pressure of her cousin's hand. At times our need for a sympathetic gesture is so great that we care not exactly what it signifies or how much we may have to pay for it afterwards. Miss Bartlett, by this timely exercise of her muscles, gained more than she would have got in hours of preaching or cross-examination.

It is clear by this point in the novel that preaching and cross-examining are exactly what Charlotte *would* have done, had Lucy resisted—and it is also clear that, given a little more time, Lucy might well have done so, as her feelings towards Miss Bartlett are none too cordial. However, she is confused and terrified, and the act of sheltering together—literally as well as symbolically under her cousin's protection—overwhelms her own inclinations in the matter. Hours later, Lucy remains entirely pliant to Charlotte's will: "Lucy obeyed. She was in her cousin's power."

Night Flight, or, the second umbrella-ing

When it is not broadcasting Mr B's nationality and socio-economic status to all and sundry, the eponymous white umbrella of Brian Sewell's novel also plays a symbolic role in the relationship between Mr B and his donkey. After a few days of slow, uncomfortable progress, keenly reminded of the enormity of the task ahead of him, Mr B very nearly abandons his donkey to her fate:

> When he saw a bus destined for Karachi, Pakistan's chief seaport, where he could so easily take a plane to London, the impulse to board it and leave Pavlova where she stood with her saddlebags and sheepskin was, for a moment, irresistible.

However, the moment passes, and "with reinforced resolve he opened his big white umbrella and, with Pavlova's lead shortened, bringing her very close to his side, sharing the shade, they set off towards the west and the Persian border." By bringing her under his umbrella, Mr B's role as protector is firmly and finally established. He will not falter again.

In C. S. Lewis's *The Lion, the Witch and the Wardrobe* (1950)—a novel positively dripping with Christian symbolism—an act of near betrayal is heightened by the sharing of an umbrella. It is summer, and Lucy Pevensie has just discovered a snowy forest inside an old wardrobe during a game of hide-and-seek:

> As she stood . . . wondering why there was a lamp-post in the middle of a wood and wondering what to do next, she heard a pitter patter of feet coming towards her. And soon after that a very strange person stepped out from among the trees into the light of the lamp-post.
>
> He was only a little taller than Lucy herself and he carried over his head an umbrella, white with snow. From the waist upwards he was like a man, but his legs were shaped like a goat's (the hair on them was glossy black) and instead of feet he had goat's hoofs. He also had a tail, but Lucy did not notice this at first because it was neatly caught up over the arm that held the umbrella so as to keep it from trailing in the snow.

After establishing that Lucy is, in fact, human, the faun asks her back to his cave for a meal with "a roaring fire—and toast—and sardines—and cake." She accepts, and he invites her into the shelter of his umbrella: "'If you will take my arm, Daughter of Eve,' said Mr Tumnus, 'I shall be able to hold the umbrella over both of us.'"

After the meal the guilt-stricken faun reveals his great betrayal: he had intended to abduct Lucy and take her to the White Witch, the evil sorceress ruling over the land. He cannot go through with it, and promises to take her back to the lamp-post so she can find her way home. "They both got up and left the tea-things on the table, and Mr Tumnus once more put up his umbrella and gave Lucy his arm, and they went out into the snow." The journey back paints a markedly different picture to their first one, for this time the faun is genuinely protecting her: "they stole along as quickly as they could, without speaking a word, and Mr Tumnus kept to the darkest places." This umbrella-ing is the faun's first true act of companionship, and he remains Lucy's firm friend and trusted advisor for years to come. In fact, the umbrella was instrumental in the inception of the story: in his essay "It All Began with a Picture . . . " (1960), C. S. Lewis explains how the plot of *The Lion, the Witch and the Wardrobe* started with an image in his head, "a picture of a faun carrying an umbrella and parcels in a snowy wood."

Some of Charles Dickens's most personal and evocative writing may be found in his essay "Please to Leave Your Umbrella" (1858). The piece is a sharply worded meditation on self-identity (more on that soon) laced with the dreamy associations of the "little reason" he is carrying around "in [his] bosom" (this "little reason" is considered by critics to be an allusion to the actor Ellen Ternan, with whom he was passionately in love). The essay concludes with the narrator and his little reason walking away beneath the protective canopy of his umbrella:

> I gave back my ticket, and got back my Umbrella, and then I and my little reason went dreaming away under its shelter through the fast-falling spring rain, which had a sound in it that day like the rustle of the coming summer.

John Bowen notes that this is the only time the narrator and the little reason are portrayed together (rather than in his bosom). He also notes, rather waggishly, that this is a very rare instance in Dickens of an umbrella being put to its proper use (further uses will be discussed shortly).

Sheltering and shielding are admirable qualities both, but—as

A king's grave in Central Africa

hinted earlier with the shadow of the king's umbrella—it is the shade
of an umbrella that is most richly invested with meaning. Amongst
the ancient Egyptian hieroglyphs there is one shaped like an umbrella ☂, roughly translating to "shadow." Sometimes it was used to
denote sovereignty – the aforementioned shadow of the king's power
or protection—but it also referred to the shadow of a person—their
khabit or *khaibit*. The *khaibit* was thought to be the source of one's
regenerative powers—for it was believed that the body, once resur-
rected after death, could not be complete without its shadow.

Accordingly, whether incorporated into the architecture of Indian
tombs as a representation of heaven or placed on the graves of de-

Woman holding an umbrella, eighth century B.C.E.

ceased chiefs in Borneo to, as Crawford puts it, "keep the dead man's spirit dry," umbrellas have had a long association with death throughout many cultures. The ancient Indian epic *Mahabharata* describes a parasol-filled royal funeral: "The litter on which was placed the lifeless body of the monarch Pandou was adorned with a flywhisk, a fan and a parasol. As music played, hundreds of men offered . . . flywhisks and parasols." In a fitting echo of his birth story, the body of Buddha was said to be shaded by canopies and parasols at his funeral procession in 487 B.C.E. In Africa, members of the Ashira tribe made advance arrangements for umbrellas to be placed over their graves, and 150 years ago umbrella-forms could still be seen shading burial grounds in Cape Coast Castle (a port for transatlantic slave trade in what is now Ghana).

However, the shadow meanings of umbrellas do not stop at death but continue through it towards regeneration and its earthly corollary, reproduction. In many cultures, particularly in India and ancient Greece, the umbrella has been closely associated with deities connected with fertility and the harvest. Amongst the most significant and best known of these are Demeter and Persephone, both associated with harvest prosperity. Octave Uzanne reports in *The Sunshade, the Glove, the Muff* (1883) that women would carry sunshades and baskets during festivals honouring both of these goddesses. According to Crawford, Persephone, who symbolized the vegetation that dies in winter and is reborn in spring, is frequently depicted on vases with an umbrella in hand.

Umbrellas were likewise wielded by the followers of the Greco-Roman god Bacchus, who was connected with death, resurrection and (re)productivity. These followers—the Bacchantes—were so debauched in their celebrations that for a long time the umbrella came to be regarded as an erotic symbol, an association that lasted until around the fifth century B.C.E., when the umbrella's status slowly began to subside into that of quotidian sunshade. In "Parasols in Etruscan Art," Jean M. Turfa notes the links between "light, death and wedding imagery" on Roman sarcophagi. In one example, a parasol is held over Ariadne as she travels with Bacchus, her husband-to-be; since she must die in order to achieve immortality, "her funeral and wedding are practically the same." Umbrellas and canopies have since featured heavily in wedding ceremonies from many cultures, held over the heads of brides, grooms or both in various Hindu, African, Jewish (in the form of the *chuppah*) and early English traditions.

Crawford notes that both the French and German verbs "to shadow"—*ombrager* and *beschatten*—once referred to the way the bull "covered" the cow during intercourse. This casts an interesting light on a passage in *The Unbearable Lightness of Being* by Milan Kundera (1984), in which the author asks:

> But is heaviness truly deplorable and lightness splendid?
>
> The heaviest of burdens crushes us, we sink beneath it, it pins us to the ground. But in the love poetry of every age, the woman longs to be weighed down by the man's body. The heaviest of burdens is therefore simultaneously an image of life's most intense fulfillment.

The erotic parallels between heaviness (lack of lightness) and shadow (lack of light) are delicate yet inescapable.

Although not widely considered the sexiest, or most romantic, of objects today, the umbrella has nevertheless accumulated various erotic charges throughout history. Ovid, in *Ars Amatoria*, or *The Art of Love* (published circa 2 C.E.) instructed his male readers to

> *Yourself hold up her parasol outspread,*
> *Yourself through crowds make clear her path ahead.*

This was a revolutionary idea at the time, for carrying a woman's umbrella was typically the duty of a slave. Michael Drayton's *The Muses Elizium* (1630) has a lover offering a pair of doves to act as umbrellas:

> *Of doves I have a dainty pair,*
> *Which, when you please to take the air,*
> *About your head shall gently hover,*
> *Your clear brow from the sun to cover;*
> *And with their nimble wings shall fan you,*
> *That neither cold nor heat shall tan you;*
> *And like umbrellas, with their feathers*
> *Shield you in all sorts of weathers.*

John Bowen finds a great deal of the erotic about Charles Dickens's umbrellas, particularly in *Nicholas Nickleby*'s Henrietta Petowker, who "knows that she is admired at the theatre by the jauntily phallic appearance of 'a most persevering umbrella in the upper boxes'" and the forbidding Wackford Squeers, who—admittedly under the influence—shares his bed with his umbrella. Bowen refers particularly to the "probing ability" of many umbrellas wielded by Dickens's women—not least Mrs Gamp—and references Jacques Derrida's description, in *Spurs: Nietzsche's Styles* (1978), of the umbrella as a "hermaphroditic spur . . . of a phallus which is modestly enfolded in its veils," symbolically not only ren-

dering the umbrella simultaneously masculine and feminine but giving it a hefty sexual charge to boot. It is Dickens's most sexually knowing women, Bowen argues, who from behind the "veils" of their skirts manipulate closed umbrellas (which, owing to construction techniques in Dickens's time, looked considerably more phallic than the slim, tapering umbrellas we know today): Mrs F's aunt in *Little Dorrit* rubbing "her esteemed insteps with her umbrella"; *Bleak House*'s Mrs Bagnet repeatedly giving Trooper George "a great poke between the shoulders with her umbrella"; and of course Mrs Gamp, a proud owner of an umbrella whose ferrule is at one point described as a "nozzle"—an object best known, as Bowen drily notes, for squirting.

Amongst the proliferation of umbrelliferous essays and stories in Victorian magazines, Ariel Beaujot notes a propensity for love stories involving umbrellas, typically of the damsel-in-distress variety, in which a stranded woman is rescued from a drenching by an eligible man, umbrella in hand. In one story, a banker "owed an excellent wife to the interposition of an umbrella," while romance flowers beneath the canopy of another on a rainy day: "'My little queen!' whispered the man, 'how fortunate it was that I brought my umbrella! Otherwise I might never have gained you for my wife.'"

Far predating British love affairs with (or beneath) the brolly are those that appear in Japanese art. In *Rain and Snow: The Umbrella in Japanese Art* (1993), Julia Meech explains the "intrigue and passion" connected with visual depictions of the objects:

> In the Edo period courtesans en route to an assignation
> seemed even more beautiful against the backdrop of
> a gorgeous janome,[20] and women were shown leaping
> from great heights to prove their love, with only an open

---

20 A "snake eye" umbrella, so named for the insert of contrasting paper circling the umbrella's apex, creating the impression, when viewed from above, of a reptilian eye.

Suzuki Harunobu's *Young Woman Jumping from the Kiyomizu Temple Balcony with an Umbrella as a Parachute*, 1765

umbrella to slow their descent. Nothing was more affecting than a man and woman walking together holding between them the stick of a single umbrella.

The umbrella jump is a particularly curious phenomenon. In the 1760s, at least four different artists produced prints depicting a woman leaping from a high place—often a temple—with just an umbrella to break her fall. Apparently the jump served as a litmus test for the future of a love affair—if the woman landed unharmed, "happiness was assured" (although it does seem a somewhat self-fulfilling prophesy; happiness doesn't usually proceed from snapped ankles or shattered pelvises). Meech notes a particularly interesting detail, visible in the image on the previous page: curled bare toes, in Japanese prints, also carried sexual connotations.

Will Self's *Umbrella* sizzles with erotic potentialities, not least in this early rain-drenched scene between Stanley and his future lover Adeline:

> ... her dress was saturated, the fabric clinging to her breasts, her belly ... *her thighs.* Stanley could not forebear from noticing that there were *no stays or lets or hindrances* ... she put up her parasol ... and under this glossy shell they ... made for the house.

When Stanley's sister Audrey lies, postcoital, with her lover Gilbert, watching people walk along High Holborn with their umbrellas, she tells him about the day when, at fourteen, she walked in on her father in flagrante with a sex worker for the benefit of an early-twentieth-century pornographer. Not batting an eyelid, her father rearranges himself, bids adieu to both cameraman and actress and fetches his umbrella before shepherding Audrey from the room. Gilbert asks her why she has suddenly recalled that day: "'[I]sh it becaushe we have jusht ... fucked?' No, she says eventuu ally, 'no, Gilbert, ... it's ... it's the umbrellas.'"

4 ‖ THE GENDERED BROLLY

THESE EROTIC UMBRELLA-RELATED interactions are performative not only of love and desire but of an exclusive heteronormativity. After several years of reading on high alert for umbrellas, I am yet to come across a single homoerotic brolly. This may reflect bias at a number of levels, including my own reading, or the paucity of gay relationships in the literary "canon" (and even that of more contemporary novels). It could well be that umbrella eroticism has weakened over time and is consequently being used less as a literary device. The elderly Iris Chase Griffen, in Margaret Atwood's *The Blind Assassin* (2000), observes that her granddaughter would "scorn umbrellas; the young like their heads to be whipped about by the elements, they find it bracing." Perhaps umbrellas are sufficiently quotidian that the image of two lovers huddled beneath one—the stuff of classic movies and vintage photographs, with all the emphasis on the tired tropes of (hetero-) romance that the context implies—is simply too steeped in traditional gender roles to be of much interest when it comes to "queering" the brolly.

OPPOSITE: Suzuki Harunobu's eighteenth-century print
Correspondence of Rajomon, in which a woman coquettishly
plays with the tip of a man's . . . umbrella

While traditions may have changed, depending on time, place and cultural context, there is evidence of strong gendered brolly affiliations going back millennia—and, indeed, right through to the present day.

Of course, roll an umbrella (or parasol) up and you have an instant gendered symbol; the phallic appearance of umbrellas has been pointedly alluded to in many literary and artistic contexts (although Derrida, as mentioned earlier, has a much more nuanced take on it, finding hermaphroditism where most see a straightforward representation of masculinity). In one of the best-known lines of *Les Chants de Maldorer* (1868–1869) the Comte de Lautréamont describes a young man as "fair . . . as the chance meeting on a dissecting-table of a sewing machine and an umbrella!" Several decades later, this fragment would inspire writers and artists of the Dada movement, who admired its surrealism and disguised sexual connotations (the male umbrella meeting the female sewing machine on the "bed" of a dissecting table, which Man Ray referenced in his 1920 sculpture *L'Enigme d'Isidore Ducasse*).

The gendering of umbrellas, however, is far more complex than—to put it bluntly—a standard dick joke. It is here that the distinction between umbrellas and parasols becomes particularly acute. Charles Dickens, in "Umbrellas," described the parasol as "the lady sister of the umbrella," while Emily Dickinson goes one step further with her poem "The Parasol Is the Umbrella's Daughter":

> *The parasol is the umbrella's daughter,*
> *And associates with a fan*
> *While her father abuts the tempest*
> *And abridges the rain.*
>
> *The former assists a siren*
> *In her serene display;*
> *But her father is borne and honored,*
> *And borrowed to this day.*

Note the paternalism, the human gender stereotypes reinforced in the anthropomorphized objects: the "honored" male as defender and protector, brave battler against the elements; the female associations with delicate, flirtatious objects (fans) and mute performance ("serene display"). The gendered implication that the umbrella, as the father, came into the world first runs counter to the history of both devices; as we have seen, the parasol predates the brolly by milb lennia.

And while the ubiquitous black pop-up brolly of today perhaps wouldn't seem to betray any allegiance to one gender or another, one need only step through the door of James Smith & Sons to witness the results of a long history of umbrella-related gender segregation. Turn left, and you can peruse a selection of dainty, betasseled umbrellas with slim spikes, elegant handles (carved dogs' heads feature frequently) and sumptuous fabrics. Turn right, and you find a much larger selection of much larger brollies: stout handled and eminently practical; taller, broader, sturdier, with not a tassel to be seen. While there's nothing to stop anyone of any gender buying any umbrella they like, there are few options for the lady who would like a slim handle on a tall umbrella with an expansive canopy, say, or the gentleman who prefers lipstick pink fabric for a modestly proportioned, crocodile-headed specimen—save to have one made specially.

Fox Umbrellas—the very same Fox responsible for Mr Fox's Paragon frame back in the nineteenth century—likewise divide stheir offerings into ladies' and gentlemen's categories: slender and betasseled, with the option of deep frills and pastel-coloured handles on the one hand; stout and unadorned with a variety of wooden handles on the other. Another of England's oldest umbrella purveyors, the luxuriously appointed Swaine Adeney Brigg, also deals in gender tropes—if somewhat less overtly. Their modest in-store selection may appear more androgynous than Smith's or Fox's, but a quick glance at their website speaks volumes about their target market, with taglines like "No self-respecting gentleman would carry anything else" and "Umbrella's [sic] fit for a prince."

To be fair to these traditional manufacturers—and to generations of socially appointed arbiters of gender roles in umbrella use
and manufacture—it is difficult to think of an object, whether func-
tional or fashionable, that hasn't at one point or another been associated with or marketed towards a specific gender. Objects as basic as
shaving gel, tissues and razors, and as diverse as books, music and
movies, continue to undergo the treatment to this day.

Moreover, as Cynthia Barnett explains in a fascinating chapter
of *Rain: A Natural and Cultural History*, even the rain itself has been
gendered throughout human history. Associations between rain
and masculinity date back at least as far as one of humankind's
oldest known gods: the bull-riding, lightning bolt–brandishing
Mesopotamian rain god called Iškur by the Sumerians, and Adad
by the Akkadians. As Barnett explains, newly settled agricultural-
ists were probably more invested in rain than any humans before
them:

> In regions . . . where agriculture depended more on rain
> than on irrigation, storm gods ranked as the most prom-
> inent of all gods . . . Still thought of as paeans to fertility,
> they came to conjure life along with rains when they felt
> appeased—droughts and floods with infertility when
> angry.

Storm gods would continue to be associated with bulls for centuries to come—partly for the distant-thunder rumble of their hoofs,
and partly for their associations with masculinity and sexual power. While rain goddesses were not unheard of, Barnett notes that
they typically functioned as the "arm candy" of the neolithic storm
gods—pleasing escorts, rather than effectual players in the rain
game.

Thanks, in part, to traditions like these, many cultures linked
the life-giving properties of rain with semen: Barnett mentions

farmers and their wives making love in the fields in the hope of bringing rain, and naked ladies sent into the fields "to sing ribald songs to the rain" (I can't quite decide whether the idea of women seducing clouds is endearingly sweet or eminently creepy: a kind of pluvial *bukkake*, if you will). Interestingly, Native Americans regard heavy rain as male, while gentle rain is considered female. Barnett notes that the Sanskrit word for rain—*varsha*—evolved from the older *vrish*, which carries connotations of "manly power" and "generative vigour." In Jewish tradition, rain is male, while its, erm, *receptacles*—lakes and rivers—are female. Rivers are likewise identified as female by Hindu people, and may even be described as pregnant during monsoonal flooding.

Little wonder, then, that umbrellas and parasols came to acquire a certain amount of gender baggage. In ancient Rome and Greece, parasol use was typically confined to women—more spepcifically to their slaves, who were charged with holding them. As far back as 520 B.C.E., Anacreon's *Ap Athenaeus* contains a reference to someone called Artamon, who is being mocked for using a parasol "as do women." In Henri Estiennes's *Dialogues* of 1578, a certain Celtophile poses this question:

> Have you seen a device which certain persons of rank in Spain and Italy carry, or have carried, less to protect themselves against flies than against the sun? It is supported upon a stick, and it is so constructed that it takes up little room when it is folded; but when it is needed, it can be opened forthwith and spread out in a round that can well cover three or four persons.

Philansone answers that he has never seen one, "but if French women saw men carrying them, they would consider them effeminate."

According to Crawford, "all the evidence" points to women being the first users of the waterproof umbrella in England—a fact that goes a long way towards explaining early reluctance among men to adopt the brolly. As John Newton (slave-trader-cum-abolitionist and composer of "Amazing Grace") remarked back in the eighteenth century, "To carry an umbrella without any headgear placed a fellow in a social no-man's land in the category of one hurrying round to the corner shop for a bottle of stout on a rainy day at the behest of a nagging landlady."

In *Trivia: or The Art of Walking the Streets of London* (1716), John Gay makes it crystal clear who is expected to wield the brolly— women, or else their slaves:

> *Good housewives all the winter's rage despise*
> *Defended by the riding-hood's disguise,*
> *Or, underneath th'umbrellas oily shed*
> *Safe thro' the wet on clinking pattens tread.*[21]
> *Let Persian dames th'umbrella's ribs display,*
> *To guard their beauties from the sunny ray;*
> *Or sweating slaves support the shady load,*
> *When Eastern monarchs show their state abroad.*
> *Britain in winter only shows its aid*
> *To guard from chilly showers the walking maid.*

The act of teasing someone reveals a great deal about social norms, and this advertisement from the December 12, 1709, issue of *The Female Tatler* is no exception:

> The young gentleman borrowing the Umbrella belonging to Wills' Coffee-house, in Cornhill, of the mistress, is hereby advertised, that to be dry from head to foot on the like occasion, he shall be welcome to the maid's pattens.

---

21 *Pattens*: protective, often heeled, overshoes used from the Middle Ages until the early twentieth century—once muddy roads and footpaths had largely been replaced with paving.

In "Text and Imagery in Suffrage Propaganda," Norman Watson suggests that the power and potential violence represented by umbrellas in antisuffrage propaganda reflected the threat felt by some men at the prospect of greater equality between the sexes.

As we have seen, however, at some point during the nineteenth century the roles reversed. The umbrella was no longer the sole preserve of women, and it became increasingly respectable for gentlemen to sport one—indeed, by Leonard Bast's time, an umbrella was nothing short of a necessary staple of a man's attire. Concomitant with this reversal came a rise in the popularity of the parasol, which established the gender binary between (male) umbrellas and (female) parasols that would persist for nearly two centuries.

In the hands of middle- and upper-class ladies, parasols became increasingly ornate, adorned with lace, fringes and embroidery. Their sticks grew ever longer and were carved of mother-of-pearl, rhinoceros horn, ivory or ebony. Handles were made of porcelain, encrusted with precious jewels or carved to resemble lions, dragons, horses or greyhounds. Large porcelain knobs, brocaded silk, feathers, ribbons and bows all made appearances. The "La Sylphide" parasol, introduced in 1844, could be opened and closed with a single button on the handle, making it a highly desirable, if costly, article (indeed, a humble seamstress in *Memoirs of an Umbrella* moves heaven and earth to carry one on her wedding day). In 1851 the French parasol-maker René-Marie Cazal wrote "Historical and Anecdotal Essay on the Umbrella, Parasol and Walking-Stick and their Fabrication," in which he extols the parasol's ability to enhance feminine charms:

> The parasol, like a rosy vapour, attenuates and softens a woman's features, it restores her faded colouring, sheltering her face with diaphanous reflections ... under its rosy or azure dome, passion is born, broods or blossoms ... How many sweet smiles have played under its Corolla! How many charming signs of the head, how many intoxicating and magic looks?

Indeed, parasols played a key role in Victorian women's fashion. In *Art in Ornament and Dress* (1877), Charles Blanc described the sunshade as "another weapon of coquetry," used by women to flirt with, tease and attract the attentions of men. But skilful handling is only one part of the picture. Along with the considerable financial pressure on women to marry came the social pressure to look "marriageable"—that is to say, youthful—for as long as possible. As discussed earlier, the use of parasols helped to maintain pale, unweathered and eminently imperial complexions, but a carefully chosen parasol could go even further by casting a bloom of youth across a woman's features. It worked quite well, if the lyrics from a song of the time, "The Parasol Parade," are to be believed:

> *At the seaside there's the girl that's rather haughty*
> *On the prom there she will roam,*
> *Well, when I say a girl, she's nearly forty,*
> *And she looks it when at home;*
> *But see her strolling out beneath a sunshade,*
> *She looks charming—simply grand—*
> *Though really her complexion*
> *Is the pink and white reflection*
> *Of the sunshade that she carries in her hand.*

To assist young and not-so-young females with their complexions, Charles Blanc included some helpful instructions on the proper application of coloured parasols. In his opinion, ideal shades included *rose de chine* or carnation silk, while anything purple, red or brown was to be absolutely avoided. Blanc advised women to resist the temptation of matching their parasol fabric to their dress if the dress were an unflattering colour for the complexion: "A pretty woman will never sacrifice her beauty, even to the rules of optical harmony."

By the earliest decades of the twentieth century parasol fashion had reached new heights of flashy absurdity. Fashion houses and individuals alike created ever more fantastic and eye-catching concoctions—so eye-catching, in fact, that it was the unspoken rule

THE SEASON'S SUNSHADES

A parasol advertisement from 1909

at polo matches to hide the parasols at start of play, so as not to spook the horses with the array of ribbons, feathers and bright colours on display. In 1922, the dog parasol became popular. Originally the term simply referred to parasols with elaborately carved dog-headed handles—but when the Pekingese and French Bulldog clubs exhibited at the Horticultural Hall that year, miniature parasols were produced to shelter the pedigree hounds.[22] By this time, however, the parasol's popularity had reached its zenith. The emerging mania for sun bathing and tanned skin ensured that the parasol quickly became outmoded.

And the umbrella? There was a raft of gimmicky inventions in the first half of the nineteenth century, including umbrellas with hollow handles for holding perfumes or writing materials; umbrellas with curtained covers; umbrellas with flasks in the handles for collecting water from the covers; umbrellas with one elongated side for covering a lady's bustle; umbrellas with windows; umbrellas with sponges attached to the tip of each rib; and umbrellas that whistled when opened. One model, called the "rhabdoskidophoros," featured a cover and ribs that folded away inside the stick to create a walking cane. But, as a Victorian writer in *The Gentleman's Magazine* rather tersely reminds us, these inventions were the exception rather than the rule:

> Yet the proprietors of such fanciful gewgaws as folding umbrellas, umbrella walking-sticks, pocket umbrellas

---

22   If you were about to scoff, don't: dog umbrellas Remain A Thing to this very day.

and the like are few and far between. They are either inventors seeking gratuitous advertisement for the off-spring of their brains, or creatures who, without their wits, and with a superfluity of vanity, angle for a cheap notoriety in the exhibitions of an eccentric appendage.

The entrepreneurial penchant for "fanciful gewgaws" (Folding umbrellas? Pocket umbrellas? What *was* the world coming to?) had largely disappeared by the second half of the nineteenth century, and the brolly remained overwhelmingly plain. By the end of World War II, umbrella production had come to a near-complete standstill, and once it revived, umbrellas were marketed to men and women alike—although, as James Smith and sundry other umbrella-makers remind us, gendered designs remain common.

Even the conditions of brolly production have seen a gender divide throughout history. When Dickens was writing his essay about umbrellas and their manufacture, the work of umbrella-making was highly specialized and specifically gendered. Before factory production became widespread, umbrellas were produced in discrete stages: first, the frames were assembled; next, they were covered with fabric; and finally, handles and ferrules were affixed. Each of these stages was conducted in separate locations by distinct groups of people with their own specific skill sets. As Dickens reports in "Umbrellas," the frame assembly was performed "by small masters in London, who [employed] lads to assist them"; the covering was "the work of women and girls at their own humble homes"; while the affixing of handles and ferrules largely happened in warehouses.

While the umbrella-frame-makers were paid three farthings per frame, the umbrella-frame-coverers were given a penny to fourpence[23] each, "according to the quality and the amount of labour." This is certainly more than the frame-makers received, but

---

23 The same approximate process as before yields conversions of between £0.46 and £1.90 in today's economy.

Dickens does not elaborate on the process of covering umbrellas or the time involved as he does with the making of the frames—perhaps because the intricacies of threading so many component parts together into a functioning machine appeared more impressive than those of sewing covers onto the frame, or perhaps because he could not, with propriety, ask for access to the "humble homes" of the women and girls who did this work. In any case, we can safely assume that the minute needlework necessary for creating individual, rib-sized sleeves and stretching the oiled fabric across these idiosyncratic frames—maintaining the correct tension across the structure and, particularly in the case of parasols, ensuring an aesthetically pleasing result—was at least as fiddly and time-consuming as the work done by the masters and their boys. Audrey Death, typist for Thomas Ince & Coy, is certainly under no illusions regarding the nature of female employment: her work is "women's work: *sweated, menial, repetitive.*"

5 ‖ A HAT WITH A HANDLE

IN MANY CULTURES, the social rules and conventions of umbrella use, no matter how rigidly coded, have ultimately decayed or completely fallen away. The veneration, or abhorrence, once attached to the objects gradually weakened, production was industrialized and—with varying degrees of enthusiasm and resistance—the objects were embraced, becoming ever more commonplace and affordable, to the point where, today, one may be purchased with an assortment of loose change at the nearest pound store.

Much as umbrella use has been democratized over time, so too have people's conceptions of themselves. Over the centuries, humanity has become far less reliant on the shelter of gods and kings. The period of the Enlightenment saw European ideas of selfhood shift dramatically. Where once people saw themselves as the playthings of gods and circumstance—in need of shielding and shelter from the flux and chaos about them—changes in Western thought and reasoning shifted to centre on the individual. That individual—brolly in hand—will be the focus of this chapter.

OPPOSITE: Print by Katsushika Hokusai (1760–1849) titled
Travelers in the Snow: a portable roof, a small snowless space
carved from the storm

It is time to look at the umbrella as an experience—the intensely solitary experience of standing beneath a brolly in the rain. For an umbrella is not just shelter, shadow, shield or an archaic indicator of gender or socioeconomic status. An umbrella is your own fragment of roof. In an ancient Chinese legend, dated to 1000 B.C.E., the wife of a skilled carpenter named Lou-Pan says, "You make houses with extreme cleverness, but they can't move; the object I'm making for personal use can be carried any distance"—and she holds up a parasol.

An umbrella's protective capacity is not only symbolic but also highly practical, and is doubtless the chief reason why umbrella use became so common, against all previous objections of sanctity, society and status. Which brings us back to Robinson Crusoe's umbrella. Robert Louis Stevenson may have joked that it was Crusoe's "civilized mind trying to express itself under adverse circumstances," but Defoe's wording leaves little doubt about the true purpose of Crusoe's laborious contraption:

> After this I spent a great deal of Time and Pains to make me an Umbrella; I was indeed in great want of one, and had a great Mind to make one; I had seen them made in the Brasils, where they are very useful in the great Heats which are there. And I felt the Heats every jot as great here . . . besides, as I was oblig'd to be much abroad, it was a most useful thing to me, as well for the Rains as the Heats. I took a world of Pains at it, and was a great while before I could make any thing likely to hold; nay, after I thought I had hit the Way, I spoil'd 2 or 3 before I made one to my Mind; but at last I made one that answer'd indifferently well: The main Difficulty I found was to make it let down. I could make it to spread, but if it did not let down too, and draw in, it was not portable for me any Way but just over my Head, which wou'd not do. However, at last, as I said, I made one to answer, and covered it with Skins, the Hair

Crusoe and his umbrella-awning

upwards, so that it cast off the Rains like a Penthouse, and kept off the Sun so effectually, that I could walk out in the hottest of the Weather with greater Advantage than I could before in the Coolest, and when I had no need of it, cou'd close it and carry it under my Arm.

The word "penthouse" now most commonly refers to rooftop apartments, but the traditional meaning is that of an awning, a canopy or a sloping roof attached to the side of a building for protection against the weather. I am yet to come across an umbrella reference that so explicitly draws the connection between umbrellas and roof structures.[24]

---

24 On the subject of structures, members of the botanical family *Umbelliferae* (or *Apiaceae*) are characterized by their distinctively shaped flower heads—namely, the umbel, an inflorescence composed of flower stalks radiating out from a central stem like the spokes of an umbrella. As with the umbrella, "*Umbelliferae*" is derived from the Latin *umbella* ("parasol") and refers to a multitude of well-known plants including carrot, celery, cumin, parsley, dill, coriander and . . . hemlock.

Hemlock.

Conium maculatum.

UMBELLIFERÆ.

Indeed, later in the book Crusoe directly compares the two, fixing his umbrella to his canoe to "keep the Heat of the Sun off of me like an Auning." Nor are we left in any doubt of its indispensability, for he considers it "the most necessary thing I had about me, next to my gun."

If we see the umbrella as a kind of roof, and we understand a "room" to be the sheltered, delineated space beneath a roof that one can inhabit, personalize and to some extent control the conditions of, then the space beneath the umbrella may be seen as a kind of portable room. In these temporary shelters one creates a fleeting room of one's own, protected from the external conditions by a personal canopy interposed between the self and the outer world. In the simple act of putting up an umbrella, then, one transitions from outside to inside—where the soft sough/hissy spit of rain on the canopy is reminiscent of that on the roof or windows of one's own home—without moving so much as a foot. Film director Woody Allen—an avid pluviophile—has explained what it is that he loves about rain:

> People are confined to their households. They seek shelter. They succor inside their houses. They run from the outside to the inside to protect themselves. They go inward and move inward.

This inwardness that rain evokes is key to an understanding of an umbrella as a room-like space into which one withdraws, and willfully cuts oneself off in several fundamental ways from the outside world.

As in a room, it becomes all too obvious when your umbrella's roof leaks, and what is supposed to stay outside becomes inside's unwelcome guest. This is illustrated in the very first pages of Graham Greene's novel *The End of the Affair* (1951), when, on a "black, wet

OPPOSITE: Hemlock, or poison parsley

night . . . in 1946," Maurice Bendrix decides to venture to his local pub for a drink:

> The little crowded hall was full of strangers' hats and coats and I took somebody else's umbrella by accident . . . Directly I began to cross the Common I realized I had the wrong umbrella, for it sprang a leak and the rain ran down under my macintosh collar.

Like a room, an umbrella is a space one can retreat within, to avoid interacting with others. As Bendrix crosses the common beneath somebody else's leaky umbrella, he sees Henry Miles—with whose wife Bendrix once had a passionate affair—walking in his direction. Bendrix describes how he could have passed Henry by under the cover of his umbrella:

> I could so easily have avoided him; he had no umbrella and . . . his eyes were blinded with the rain . . . If I had walked straight by him, he wouldn't have seen me, and I could have made certain by stepping two feet off the pavement.

Of course, Bendrix does not do this, for if he had, the novel would have unfolded quite differently—or not at all.

Lucy Honeychurch enacts her own retreat in *A Room With a View*, although for very different reasons. In one of the most comic moments of the book, set some time after Lucy's trip to Italy, Miss Honeychurch and her mother are enjoying a quiet stroll with Lucy's fiancé when they are interrupted by the sudden appearance of three naked men, one of them her old paramour, George, who

> whooped in their faces, turned, and scudded away down the path to the pond, still clad in Mr Beebe's hat.

"Gracious alive!" cried Mrs Honeychurch, "Who ever were those unfortunate people?"

... Lucy ... was all parasol.

Perhaps the most beautiful expression of umbrella interiority I've encountered comes from Stephan Köhler's "Parents of Private Skies," an essay about the dying craft of umbrella manufacture in Japan, where cheap, synthetic Western umbrellas have all but edged out traditional oiled bamboo-and-paper models. After visiting the elderly craftspeople and watching their precise, expert work, Köhler purchases a model of his own to take away with him.

> I carefully opened my new umbrella. When it was finally fully extended, I found myself surrounded by smells of oil, bamboo and lacquer, the whispering of raindrops amplified a hundred times. Red light tinted my hand and probably my face. It was like being inside a room with red windows. The umbrella felt warm and kind, as if I could feel the care and serenity of the people who had made it.

He walks through streets crowded with umbrellas—but none of them are traditional Japanese models. In a society keen on conformity, he is the odd one out, and attracting attention. Uncomfortable, he retreats into the umbrella's crimson shelter.

> After a while I felt lonely, exposed as if nude, and helpless against the glances and unspoken remarks. Instead of looking at the crowd, I looked above me into the red roof suspended by myriad filigree bamboo ribs ... radiating from the stick ... reaching out for infinite points in the universe, yet all united by a yellow cotton star. I felt safe

Private sky/private sun: my own tattered parasol on an autumn afternoon

and protected again. The umbrella in my hand had become my companion. Both of us were foreigners. It was a
shield not only for the rain. It guarded my world, defined
my space. It was my private sky.

Of course, an umbrella is an imperfect room. Depending on the
size of the canopy and the persistence of the rain, being under an
umbrella can be a decidedly half-in, half-out experience. The body
undergoes a split, between what is protected and what is not. The
cosy shelteredness of the head and shoulders is often offset by the
slow seep of water into shoes, the cold cling of fabric around the ankles. This apposite example from Han Kang's *The Vegetarian* (2007)
occurs on a rainy day in South Korea:

> The raindrops drum against her umbrella, so forcefully
> it seems they might rip through the material . . . It wasn't

the kind of rain for which an umbrella could provide sufficient shelter, so her blouse and trousers are half soaked.

Nevertheless, with its invisible walls—perceptible only at the juncture of rain and not-rain—an umbrella sketches out the edges of that tenuous bubble we know as "personal space." Observe any crowded footpath on a rainy day and you will see umbrellas tilting and shifting, scooping and lifting as the spaces beneath them flex and squeeze to accommodate passersby. Or not—which brings us to an excellent scene from Milan Kundera's *The Unbearable Lightness of Being*, in which a meeting of umbrellas becomes a battle of wills amongst the women on the busy, drizzly streets of Prague.

> Arched umbrella roofs collided with one another. The men were courteous, and when passing Tereza they held their umbrellas high over their heads and gave her room to go by. But the women would not yield; each looked straight ahead, waiting for the other woman to acknowledge her inferiority and step aside . . .
>
> when [Tereza] realized her courtesy was not being reciprocated, she started clutching her umbrella like the other women and ramming it forcefully against the oncoming umbrellas. No one ever said "Sorry." For the most part no one said anything, though once or twice she did hear a "Fat cow!" or "Fuck you!" . . . Tereza recalled the days of the invasion and the girls in miniskirts carrying flags on long staffs . . . She had taken many pictures of those young women against a backdrop of tanks. How she had admired them! And now these same women were bumping into her, meanly and spitefully. Instead of flags, they held umbrellas . . . They were ready to fight as obstinately against a foreign army as against an umbrella that refused to move out of their way.

Setting some questionable gender representations to one side, the scene in this novel is an apt illustration of the highly individualized space created beneath an umbrella. Tereza had once admired the cooperation of the city's women as they banded together in a nonviolent act of resistance: the collective sexual taunting of the invaders. Without a common enemy to unite against, however, they have begun to resist each other. Each woman's space is defined by her umbrella, and each woman is determined to defend this space—in a manner that would be impossible without said umbrella.

Nor is the individuality of the umbrella-experience confined to the mere act of being beneath one. Like clothing, shoes and accessories, umbrellas can act as a powerful expression of personality—a hat with a handle, if you will.[25] Shops like James Smith & Sons carry a wealth of shapes, colours and sizes, and even—as Mr B reminds us in *The White Umbrella*—invite personal customization. And just as a character can become synonymous with their hooked hand or red riding hood, so too can one become indelibly associated with their umbrella. John Bowen calls it "umbrella style": this marriage of an individual with their brolly, whereby an umbrella becomes an extension of selfhood in the way in which it is wielded. We could also call it metonymy: see the Gamps, Robinsons and Chamberlains of centuries past.

Although their names may not have become quite so entangled with umbrella nomenclature, plenty of other characters possess strong affinities with their brollies. Mary Poppins is a perfect example: whether walking briskly through the park on errands, umbrella tucked beneath one arm, or drifting—straight-backed, booted feet turned neatly out—above Cherry Tree Lane, she is nearly impossible to picture without her umbrella.

---

25 This concept is beautifully captured within the etymology of the Japanese character for umbrella: as Julia Meech explains, *karakasa* combines the Chinese character for "hat" with another meaning "stick"—so, "hat on a stick."

So, too, is G. K. Chesterton's Father Brown. Father Brown, a priest, uses keen intuition, a knowledge of criminal behaviour (gleaned in the confessional) and his unassuming appearance to catch thieves and apprehend murderers. In the first Father Brown story, "The Blue Cross," the little priest is introduced to us through the eyes of another, whose assessment is far from favourable. Father Brown is variously described as "a very short Roman Catholic priest" with "a face as round and dull as a Norfolk dumpling" and "eyes as empty as the North Sea"; a "silly sheep" with a "mooncalf simplicity"; and someone who "might have provoked pity in anybody." He carried a "large, shabby umbrella, which constantly fell on the floor." We soon learn that much of his projected simplicity is an act designed to foil a criminal, and the sharp workings of his mind are laid bare. But the shabby umbrella remains a defining costume-piece throughout the series, and epitomizes Father Brown's presence in the world as a quiet, humble sort of person, the kind you rarely notice or think twice about—a mistake that many seasoned criminals go on to make, to their detriment.

Although Rubeus Hagrid's umbrella is not so indivisible from his character as the umbrellas carried by Father Brown and Mary Poppins, it nevertheless plays an essential function in establishing and cementing his character in his earliest appearances, particularly in his relation to the nonmagical world. Everything about Hagrid that is disturbing in the tightly controlled ordinariness of the Dursley's world—his size; his wild, disheveled looks; his poorly concealed magical abilities; his loyalty to Harry—is epitomized by his frilly pink umbrella: not only in the uses he puts it to (on which, more later) but in the way it disrupts traditional stereotypes of masculinity.

Umbrellas, needless to say, attach themselves to most characters in Will Self's *Umbrella*, but Samuel Death—Audrey and Stanley's father—is most completely and consistently associated with one.

This is done mainly by dint of a long journey through London with a young Audrey. The journey culminates in the scene at the pornographer's, which is subtly foreshadowed in the rhythmic yet curiously intimate movements of Death's umbrella (the female is described as "[fingering] the joints between the cobbles") as it taps and traces the contours of London. As previously mentioned, when Audrey recalls the scene at the end of that walk, it is not the sex that triggers the extraordinary memory of her father but the sight, through the window, of umbrellas sprouting from Holborn Underground station.

On the subject of sex, there is a subtle yet inextricable link between umbrellas, parasols and the titular character of Gustave Flaubert's 1856 masterpiece *Madame Bovary*. Early in the book, the doctor Charles Bovary is called to fix a farmer's broken leg. Over the course of several house calls, Charles slowly becomes aware of his attraction to the farmer's daughter, Emma. The reader, of course, picks up on it much quicker—alerted, in no small part, by the delin cate parasol erotics at play:

> One day, when it was thawing, the trees in the yard were oozing damp from their bark, the snow on top of the sheds was melting. She was at the door; she went to fetch her parasol, she opened it. The parasol, made of marbled silk, as the sun came shining through it, spread shifting colours over the whiteness of her face. There she was smiling in the moist warmth of its shade; and you could hear the drops of water, one by one, falling on the taut fabric.

Emma and Charles's wedding acts as the key to unlocking Emma's interiority: only once they are married do we begin to learn about her character, her dreams and her yearning for the giddy heights of emotion and experience. It is a parasol (perhaps the same parasol Charles once admired her beneath) that accompanies her earliest expression of dissatisfaction in her marriage. In fact, this is the very first time we hear her voice directly, unmodulated by the narrator or other characters:

> [S]itting on the grass, poking at it with the point of her sunshade, Emma kept saying to herself:
> —Oh, why, dear God, did I marry him?

Later in the novel Emma walks with the young clerk Monsieur Léon, her sunshade sheltering the first tender blossoming of their love for one another:

> [T]he young woman and her companion heard as they walked only the fall of their steps on the earth, the words they spoke to each other, and the whisper of Emma's dress as it swished about . . . In the brickwork, wallflowers had pushed their way up; and, with the edge of her open sunshade, Madame Bovary, as she passed, scattered a few of their faded petals into yellow dust; or else a trailing spray of honeysuckle and clematis would scratch on the silk, getting caught in the fringes.

In this, much later, scene between the two lovers, they are together beneath a canopy once more—an umbrella, this time:

> There was a thunderstorm, and they talked under an umbrella as the lightning flashed.
> Separation was becoming intolerable.

It is a significant moment in both characters' lives, for "it was then that she gave him her promise to find, no matter how, some way of seeing each other, unconstrained, at least once a week."

Flaubert did not limit his umbrella use to just the one character; casual references slip in and out across the book. But the complete association of character with umbrella is unique to Emma. All other instances are passing moments, belonging to the liturgical, mercantile or domestic spheres: the umbrella left behind by a priest; the large umbrellas sheltering the flower sellers; the bundle of umbrellas carried over the shoulder of a servant; or the crowded meadow in which "housewives bumped into you with their big umbrellas, their baskets and their youngsters." No umbrella in the book carries the erotic charge of Emma's, and it punctuates her strongest assertions of individuality.

Just as one's umbrella can reflect one's practicality, frivolity or style, it can also reveal something deeper. As Robert Louis Stevenson points out, a carelessly chosen umbrella can never tell us a great deal about a person ("for it is only in what a man loves that he displays his real nature"). But one chosen deliberately can not only betray an aspect of oneself that one would rather remain hidden but also be used to practice deceptions upon others:

> The falsity and the folly of the human race have degraded that graceful symbol to the ends of dishonesty . . . [some umbrellas], from certain prudential motives, are chosen directly opposite to the person's disposition. A mendacious umbrella is a sign of great moral degradation. Hypocrisy naturally shelters itself below a silk; while the fast youth goes to visit his religious friends armed with the decent and reputable gingham. May it not be said of the bearers of these inappropriate umbrellas that they go about the streets "with a lie in their right hand"?

For Charles Dickens, the dishonesty lay not in the act of carrying an umbrella but in leaving one behind. In 'Please to Leave Your Umbrella,' the narrator (with his "little reason") pays a visit to Hampton Court Palace, to peruse the artworks there. The narrator is asked to leave his umbrella in the foyer, a request with which he complies most willingly, "for my umbrella is very wet." He ascends the stairs and proceeds to wander the rooms above. For some time, despite his evident lack of aesthetic satisfaction, he appears to be in a state of near ecstasy:

> I wonder . . . whether, with this little reason in my bosom, I should ever want to get out of these same interminable suites of rooms, and return to noise and bustle! . . . My little reason should make of these queer dingy closet-rooms, these little corner chimney-pieces tier above tier, this old blue china of squat shapes, these dreary old state bedsteads with attenuated posts . . . an encompassing universe of beauty and happiness . . . I and my little reason . . . would keep house here, all our lives, in perfect contentment; and when we died, our ghosts should make of this dull Palace the first building ever haunted happily!

Something, however—"a stagnant pool of blacking in a frame"— calls him to his senses, and he realizes that he has left behind not only his umbrella, but also his judgment, taste and individuality along with it.

> Please to put into your umbrella . . . all your powers of comparison, all your experience, all your individual opinions. Please to accept with this ticket for your umbrella the individual opinions of some other personage . . . and to swallow the same without a word of demur. Be so good as to leave your eyes with your umbrellas, gentlemen, . . . and you shall acknowledge . . . this hideous porcelain-ware to be beautiful, these wearisomely stiff and unimaginative forms to be graceful, these coarse daubs to be masterpieces. Leave your umbrella and take up your gentility.

In this essay, the umbrella functions as an assertion of selfhood, the proof that one is a complete and well-rounded individual with one's own sense of taste, capable of independent thought. All aspects of the self, Dickens notes, that must be dispensed with in the performance of many—if not all—civil duties, may be identified with one's umbrella. He recalls similar experiences of surrendering one's judgment at the doors of churches and various public assemblages; going to a trial at the Old Bailey, where "I was requested to put so many things into it that it became, though of itself a neat umbrella, more bulgy than Mrs Gamp's"; and, worst of all, a visit to the House of Commons, where he was required to put aside "the difference between Black and White, which is really a very large one and enough to burst any Umbrella." In short, he concludes, "All through life, according to my personal experience, I must please to leave my Umbrella, or I can't go in."

This definition of Umbrella, and its strong ties to the individual, recalls those more ancient, religious understandings of the word pertaining to wholeness and unity. In this context, it is the wholeness and unity of the self that must be disrupted and laid to one side for the sake of social convention. And since the leaving of an umbrella is only done indoors, Dickens's essay introduces the idea that there exist in all buildings certain inherent social codes requiring the willful suppression of one's full individuality and better judgment. In "Please to Leave Your Umbrella," then, one is entirely free to be oneself only whilst out-of-doors, holding or inhabiting the umbrella of one's very own opinions, taste and experience.

6 ‖ FORGOTTEN OBJECTS AND FRIGHTFUL MORALITIES

WALK AROUND ANY city sufficiently blessed with rain (and, ideally, a wind tunnel or two) and you will no doubt meet, at some point on your travels, a discarded umbrella. They tend to lurk in corners and alleyways, jammed half in, half out of bins, or stuck amongst rubbish heaps awaiting collection: rain slicked, limp and melancholy objects, with bent or broken wings, spindles showing, canopies detached and flapping. Broken battered sea birds, littering the streets.

In *Bring Me Sunshine*, Charlie Connelly devotes a whole chapter to umbrellas, waxing lyrical about the "wonderful dignity" of a brolly, the "smooth, symmetrical flowering as you put it up, the effortless movement and coordination of countless working parts, the elegance of its dome." He calls umbrellas "beautiful machines" and laments "seeing one battered and ruined and shoved unceremoniously into a bin." For Connelly, the thoughtless disposal of a broken brolly is a supreme mark of disrespect for the feat of engineering—

OPPOSITE: I think this one exploded? Charing Cross Road, London

A flower behind the ear, Liverpool

the "triumph of nearly every kind of human industry"—that has gone into each one, whether it's a cheap pop-up or a distinguished safari model.

However, these discombobulated umbrellas have always struck a note of comic pathos with me. What a hapless, helpless object is the broken brolly. Some deteriorating things can be adapted for other purposes: parts salvaged, resources reappropriated. Clothing can be torn into rags, food scraps can be composted, furniture can be dismantled for hardware and timber. But a brolly, for all its possible uses in life, in death is good for very little else.[26] Unable to be mended by the layperson—and rarely worth the mending—the broken brolly is cast aside, where it cannot help but look awkward and out of place.

This note of wrong place, wrong time is a key aspect of brollyness, and one that Dickens plays to great comic effect in his umbrella writing (one is reminded, yet again, of Mrs Gamp's gamp). In "Dickens's Umbrellas," John Bowen notes an interesting example from *The Old Curiosity Shop*. The lawyer Sampson Brass is eulogizing his client, the villainous Quilp, who is believed to be dead (but is in fact listening at the keyhole). In so doing, Brass acknowledges Quilp's "wit and humour, his pathos and his umbrella." But what is an umbrella—or rather, its signifier—doing in a eulogy? As Bowen writes,

> Qualities that we might want to remember as being an essential aspect or accomplishment of the dead, such as wit, pathos and humour, are suddenly punctuated by a thing that seems merely contingent, occasional, easily detachable or lost. The umbrella . . . seems to have got itself into the wrong place.

In London, where bags of rubbish are piled on the sides of streets for nightly collection and antilittering laws seem all but nonexistent, there is no shortage of umbrellas getting themselves into the wrong places. While I was researching fictional umbrellas, I realized that I was encountering their real-life counterparts in the wild at least once a week, and made it my mission to start documenting them.

---

26 As I write, I am reminded of my friend Rachel. We were walking through Brisbane's West End in the long summer holidays. It was morning, but already the heat was rising like swarms of flies from the bitumen. Longing for rain, we were suddenly struck with the idea of making skirts from the fabric of broken umbrellas: one short skirt per brolly, or longer ones pieced together from several. We decided to start an umbrella-skirt-making collective. Like most ideas from that rich composty period of life, it never did quite eventuate.

Gutter monster, London

Just as a new word seems to proliferate in your reading the moment you learn it, the umbrellas, too, began multiplying as soon as I started looking out for them. I learned their habits as if I were tracking wild animals. I knew to keep particular watch in unused doorways—thresholds to nowhere—and down side streets and alleyways. I scrutinized every rubbish heap and odd-looking projection from bins. I learned what weather they liked best (early bluster, followed by a clear day; presumably because no one bothers persisting with a failed umbrella once the sun comes out). Soon, I was finding several per week—on one memorable occasion, four in five minutes. As I posted and shared the photos, my friends started

Broken blossom, Christmas Eve, London

sending me pictures of their own wild brolly encounters. Brollies
bred brollies bred brollies.

Most umbrellas I found were chaotically deformed, beyond
usefulness, but some were, by all appearances, simply forgotten.
A forgotten brolly has its own pathos: according to Connelly, over
eighty thousand umbrellas are left on London's public transport system every year. He writes melancholically of the "more than two
hundred discarded umbrellas a day doing endless turns around the
Circle line or ending up homeless and unloved in some floodlit bus
depot in the early hours of the morning."

Lost and forgotten umbrellas, however, are not just a contem-

Dalek, London

porary woe. As long as there have been umbrellas, there have been people to lose them and little pockets of the universe for them to disappear into. None, perhaps, knew this so well as Friedrich Nietzsche, who has perplexed generations of scholars with this one small sentence tucked amongst his unpublished manuscripts:

"I have forgotten my umbrella."

The words are neatly enclosed in quotation marks, almost as if they were the chance overhearing of a profound vocalization, or an eyebrow raised skeptically at the veracity of a statement. In his slim volume *Spurs: Nietzsche's Styles*, Jacques Derrida interrogates this sentence for every scrap of meaning, or not-meaning, it may hold, from the literal:

> Everyone knows what "I have forgotten my umbrella" means. I have . . . an umbrella. It is mine. But I forgot it.

To the referential:

> One doesn't just happen onto an unwanted object of this sort in a sewing-up machine on a castration table.

To the psychological:

> It is not only the umbrella that is recalled but also its having been forgotten.

With a passing nod to that most impressive of umbrella talents:

> An umbrella is the sort of thing that, just when it is really needed, one might either have or not have . . . Or else one still has it when it is no longer needed.

Just as umbrellas so frequently get themselves into odd places, so too has this textual fragment from a man widely regarded as one of the giants of Western philosophy. With almost palpable glee, Derrida describes the efforts of scholars to locate meaning in the text, those who think it "an aphorism of some significance" and "look for it to come from the most intimate reaches of this author's thought." But, as Derrida points out,

> in order to be so assured, one must have forgotten that it

is a text that is in question, the remains of a text, indeed a forgotten text. An umbrella perhaps. That one no longer has in hand.

Ignorant of the context in which the fragment was scribbled, clueless as to what was passing through Nietzsche's brain when first he wrote it, we can but guess at its meaning—unless, of course, we admit the possibility that the text, "in some monstrous way," may simply mean exactly what it means: Nietzsche has forgotten his umbrella. But given the impossibility of knowing, the meaning of this text—or umbrella—remains suspended in a state of comprehension yet bafflement; it is "at once open and closed, or each in turn, folded/unfolded . . . it is just an umbrella that you couldn't use."

Karl Rossman is familiar with umbrellas you can't use. In Franz Kafka's first, and unfinished, novel, *Amerika* (published post-humously in 1927), the sixteen-year-old German is about to disembark with little money and no English onto American shores, when he discovers he has left his umbrella in his cabin.

> A young man with whom he had struck up a slight acquaintance on the voyage called out in passing: "Not very anxious to go ashore, are you?"—"Oh, I'm quite ready," said Karl with a laugh, and being both strong and in high spirits he heaved his box onto his shoulder. But as his eye followed his acquaintance, who was already moving on among the others lightly swinging a walking stick, he realized with dismay that he had forgotten his umbrella down below.

He asks his friend to mind his box and heads back below, but immediately becomes lost in the labyrinthine (*Kafkaesque*, even . . .) corridors. There, he meets and befriends a stoker, who has a quarrel with a senior member of staff. Karl persuades him to take his grievances to the captain and accompanies him to the office. Once there, he has the extraordinary good fortune of meeting an uncle he had never hoped to contact and finds himself luxuriously provided for. All because of a lost umbrella (which is never, incidentally, recovered).

John Bowen observes similar patterns of loss and recovery in the work of Charles Dickens, umbrellas that stage "little . . . theatres of absence and presence." Dickens set the tone early: his very first published short story, "Mr Minns and his Cousin" (originally published as "A Dinner at Poplar Walk" in 1833) includes an umbrella that does exactly this, appearing at the beginning of the story and promptly disappearing at a vital moment. The title character, a proper and exacting middle-aged bachelor whose "love of order was as powerful as his love of life," is introduced to us as

> always exceedingly clean, precise, and tidy; perhaps somewhat priggish, and the most retiring man in the world. He usually wore a brown frock-coat without a wrinkle, light inexplicables without a spot, a neat neckerchief with a remarkably neat tie, and boots without a fault; moreover, he always carried a brown silk umbrella with an ivory handle.

Mr Minns has a cousin, Mr Octavius Budden, whom Mr Minns detests. However, Mr Minns is "godfather by proxy" to Mr Budden's son, and the Buddens invite Mr Minns to dinner, in the hope of advancing their son in the eyes of the bachelor and seeing him remembered in Mr Minns's will. The dinner is an unqualified disaster. Mr Minns cannot enjoy the raucous company of his fellow guests, much less the hospitality of his hosts. Moreover, at the end of the meal, as he tries to make a hasty escape by the last coach back to London, he finds that he has misplaced his umbrella:

But, the brown silk umbrella was nowhere to be found; and as the coachman couldn't wait, he drove back to the Swan, leaving word for Mr Minns to "run round" and catch him. However, as it did not occur to Mr Minns for some ten minutes or so, that he had left the brown silk umbrella with the ivory handle in the other coach, coming down; and, moreover, as he was by no means remarkable for speed, it is no matter of surprise that when he accomplished the feat of "running round" to the Swan, the coach—the last coach—had gone without him.

Umbrellaless on a rainy night, Mr Minns is forced to walk back to his Covent Garden flat, where he arrives—"cold, wet, cross, and miserable"—around three in the morning. The loss of the umbrella doesn't only cap off a night of displeasure for Mr Minns; it also epitomizes the threat to order and boundaries that the Budden family represents. That night, the umbrella had "got itself into the wrong place"—and so had Mr Minns.

Umbrellas slip in and out of the action in George Bernard Shaw's play *Pygmalion* (1913). Caught in a rainstorm at the theatre, Freddy Eynsford-Hill dashes off with an umbrella, knocking over a flower girl, Eliza Doolittle, and spilling her wares on the ground. Her outcry attracts the notice of Henry Higgins, and their resulting interaction precipitates the events of the play. Later, when Eliza runs away from Higgins's house and he enquires about her whereabouts at the local police station, his mother invokes the abject object-ness of lost umbrellas to chastise him:

> PICKERING. The inspector made a lot of difficulties. I really think he suspected us of some improper purpose.
> MRS HIGGINS. Well of course he did. What right have you to go to the police and give the girl's name as if she were a thief, or a lost umbrella, or something? Really!

Mr. Liston as Paul Pry. "Just looked in! — hope I don't intrude"

Paul Pry, as played by John Liston

There is a similar reference in *Howard's End*, after Leonard Bast's wife visits the Schlegels to ascertain the whereabouts of her husband:

> [T]he door was flung open, and Helen burst in in a state of extreme excitement.
>
> "Oh, my dears, what do you think? You'll never guess. A woman's been here asking me for her husband." . . .
>
> "I hope you were pleased," said Tibby.
>
> "Of course," Helen squeaked. "A perfectly delightful experience . . . she asked for a husband as if he was an umbrella. She mislaid him Saturday afternoon—and for a long time suffered no inconvenience. But all night and all this morning her apprehensions grew. Breakfast didn't seem the same—no, no more did lunch, and so she strolled up to Two, Wickham Place as being the most likely place for the missing article."

A lost umbrella features recurrently in a popular play of the nineteenth century. *Paul Pry*, written by John Poole, was a three-act farce that premiered in 1825 and was widely performed for nearly half a century, with productions staged as far afield as New York and Sydney. The eponymous (and aptly named) Pry is, in the words of one character, "one of those idle, meddling fellows, who, having no employment themselves, are perpetually interfering in other people's affairs." Paul Pry's signature move is to "forget" his umbrella at someone's house, using it as a cover to return and eavesdrop on conversations not intended for his ears. A typical exchange—usually conducted after Pry is found crouching beneath a window or by a keyhole—goes something like this:

> PRY. Beg pardon! I forgot my umbrella, that's all.
> HARDY. Plague take you, and your umbrella.

The play is referenced in G. H. Rodwell's *Memoirs of an Umbrella*, when Mr Stutters borrows Herbert Trevillian's umbrella to go to a masquerade dressed as Paul Pry. Evidence of Pry's popularity at the time (*Memoirs* was published in 1846) may be found in the guests' instantaneous reaction to Stutters's costume:

> As we went in, the people in the crowd set up a "shiloo," as they called it, for Paul Pry, and shouted out: "That's right old un: you haven't forgot your umbrella—ha, ha, ha!"

So convincingly does Mr Stutters play the part that his own umbrella suspects him of engaging his disguise for practical purposes:

> Mr Stutters did not for a moment forget his assumed character; but it having all the natural touches of a true Paul Pry, so fully developed, I began shrewdly to suspect that it was for the purpose of real Pryism he had adopted the character, rather than for mere amusement.

Of course, abandonment—by accident or design—is not the only way to lose one's umbrella. Acts of umbrella-related forgetting may apply not only to the object itself, but also to its history of ownership (one is reminded of Emily Dickinson's parting shot: "And borrowed to this day"). As nineteenth-century English dramatist Douglas Jerrold once remarked,

> There are three things that no man but a fool lends, or, having lent, is not in the most helpless state of mental crassitude if he ever hopes to get back again. These three things . . . are—BOOKS, UMBRELLAS, and MONEY!

In a time when black "city umbrellas" were carried by most genytlemen, and left dripping in umbrella-stands at the entrances to public venues, it was very easy to take another's umbrella (as Maurice Bendrix discovered, to his consternation, that rainy night on the common). Whether the taking is done by accident or design often remains undiscoverable—even, apparently, to the party who has done the taking. A. G. Gardiner (1865–1946) wrote an entire essay on the subject ("On Umbrella Morals") after his silk umbrella was "mistakenly" removed from an umbrella-stand and a baggy, cotton "abomination" left in its place. He dubbed this lapse in conscience "umbrella morals." One suffering with these

> would never put his hand in another's pocket, or forge a cheque or rob a till—not even if he had the chance. But he will swop umbrellas, or forget to return a book, or take a rise out of the railway company. In fact he is a thoroughly honest man who allows his honesty the benefit of the doubt.

According to Gardiner, even "[q]uite impeccable people, people who ordinarily seem unspotted from the world," may suffer from the affliction. This act of "[playing] hide-and-seek with our own conscience" was also remarked upon by William Sangster, who described it as the "frightful morality that exists with regard to borrowing umbrellas."

It was, presumably, in the hopes of addressing such lapses in morality that an umbrella with an unscrewable handle was invented for use in gentlemen's clubs—the theory being that nobody would want to take a handleless brolly. However, in the words of an essayist of the time, "it was felt to be an unclubable act for a man to enter his club with an umbrella that implied a distrust of the honesty of the members of his joint-stock home," and the handleless brolly never did catch on—allowing the "frightful morality" of gentlemen umbrella users to continue unchecked. G. H. Rodwell cheekily references umbrella morals in the following passage from *Memoirs of an Umbrella*:

Two or three days now passed away very quietly, when one morning, Alfred . . . remembered he had not yet returned poor me to my home, so carried me off at once to make up for his neglect, and prove that, unlike the generality of society, with respect to my species, he wished each to do as he liked with his own.

Was it frightful morality that induced Helen Schlegel to remove Leonard Bast's umbrella from the concert hall and take it home, or sheer carelessness? The sympathetic reader will err on the side of the latter; Helen's reaction to the performance of Beethoven's Fifth ("The music had summed up to her all that had happened or could happen in her career. She read it as a tangible statement, which could never be superseded . . . life could have no other meaning") betokens a certain preoccupation of mind. Whatever the motives, however, this one act is the catalyst for the entire novel.

Then, of course, there are the outright umbrella thieves. George Borrow may once have remarked that "robbers never carry umbrellas," but Roald Dahl might beg to differ. The little old man in "The Umbrella Man" is—in true Dahlian fashion—not all that he seems. "Aren't we lucky," the mother says after they swap a £1 note for the gentleman's £20 umbrella. "I've never had a silk umbrella before. I couldn't afford it." She heaps praise upon the man: "He was a gentleman . . . a *real* gentleman . . . Wealthy, too, otherwise he wouldn't have had a silk umbrella. I shouldn't be surprised if he isn't a titled person."

But her quick-witted daughter has noticed that across the street, the man is not hailing a taxi at all: he is hurrying somewhere with quick, determined footsteps. They set off in hot pursuit. He heads straight for a pub, and they watch through a window as he swaps his pound note for a triple whiskey. Then, on his way out of the pub, "in a manner so superbly cool and casual that you hardly noticed anything at all, he lifted from the coat-rack one of the many wet umbrellas hanging there, and off he went." Back on the rainy street, unaware he is being watched, he swaps his umbrella for another pound note, and heads off to a different pub. "'So that's his little game!' my mother said. 'Neat,' I said, 'Super.'"

Umbrella morality is such a well-known phenomenon that it has passed into verse, the most famous example of which is attributed to Lord Bowen:

> The rain it raineth every day
> Upon the just and unjust fella,
> But mostly on the just, because
> The unjust steals the just's umbrella.

In a passage from *Memoirs of an Umbrella*, the benefits (or not) of umbrella theft are very frankly dissected by a pair of Dickensian opportunists. On the way home from the masquerade, the narrator is accidentally dropped from a coach and lies "without help or hope, low on the highway." In due time it is picked up by a Fagin-like man and his young "apprentice," who is given the benefit of the older man's wisdom with an expert appraisal of the object's value: unlike some "humbrellas," as the man calls them, this one has no silver parts worth selling. However, the man observes that the owner's name is engraved on the handle and proposes to return it, for in so doing "we'll . . . get a reward about twice as much as we could sell it for."

In "The Philosophy of Umbrellas," Robert Louis Stevenson rather generously lays the blame for umbrella morals and/or theft on the impossibility of *not* losing one's umbrella:

> [M]en, not by nature UMBRELLARIANS, have tried again
> and again to become so by art . . . have expended their
> patrimony in the purchase of umbrella after umbrella,
> and yet have systematically lost them, and have finally,
> with contrite spirits and shrunken purses, given up their

vain struggle, and relied on theft and borrowing for the remainder of their lives.

Nowadays, in a time when most umbrellas aren't worth the stealing and are tossed aside like sweet wrappers when they fail, umbrella theft and "frightful moralities" have been largely replaced with general indifference. Like pens, plectrums and Tupperware containers, the umbrella often seems an entity that is not owned but exists in a state of flux, traveling from person to person, taken up and left behind according to various states (or absences) of mind. Think of the umbrellas doing endless loops on the Circle line, the inevitable bundles in the corner of lost property offices, the umbrellas in the staff room that nobody seems to own, or forgetting which they do own, they are afraid to take one away lest it actually belong to someone else. I would suggest that modern-day umbrella ownership has less to do with a specific object than with the category as a whole: one possesses *an* umbrella, not *their* umbrella.

A state of continual brolly flux, in which the absence of umbrellas intrudes more on human notice than their presence, reads like a textbook symptom of late capitalism. Journey back a few centuries to Edo-period Japan, however, and we find a tradition in which discarded and abandoned brollies manage not only to be noticeable, but disruptive, playful, malicious and occasionally even somewhat terrifying.

Like most monstrous creatures, the supernatural and demonic beings known in Japan as *yokai* owe their origins to the anxieties of humans in the face of darkness: of that which is known becoming foreign and unfamiliar. Yumoto Koichi explains further in the introduction to his art collection *Yokai Museum*:

> As the sun sets on the day, darkness spreads around us. The fields in which we work and play and the roads we travel back and forth on unthinkingly during the day, at

nighttime turn into pitch-black space, as if defying the control of human beings, and the sense that something is lurking in that darkness is palpable. And it's not just outside. Inside the houses of old, dimly lit with paper lanterns, the places where no human being exists are shrouded in darkness. In such places, Japanese people began to believe in presences that were beyond human understanding, causing creatures, called yokai, to be created in their minds.

Within the vast collection of yokai is a subgroup called *tsukumogami*—old and neglected household objects that, after a long period of disuse, become sentient—or, as Yumoto Koichi puts it, "ar—rogant, domineering and running wild." And amongst these wayward tsukumogami lurks—perhaps unsurprisingly—an umbrella.

According to Julia Meech, old, tattered umbrellas were often used in Japanese art to indicate the fragility and fleetingness of life. However, their ability to come alive added a further, unsettling dimension to their presence—a fact alluded to in this haiku by Yosa Buson (1716–1783):

> *Oh, the winter rain*
> *on a moonlit night*
> *when the shadow of an old umbrella shudders.*

The actor Arashi Sangorô III inscribed this poem on an image of himself playing an umbrella monster:

> *My flower umbrella*
> *tattered and worn—*
> *in the guise of a monster!*

OPPOSITE: The actor Arashi Sangorô III Utagawa Toyokuni as an umbrella ghost, or *kasa-obake*

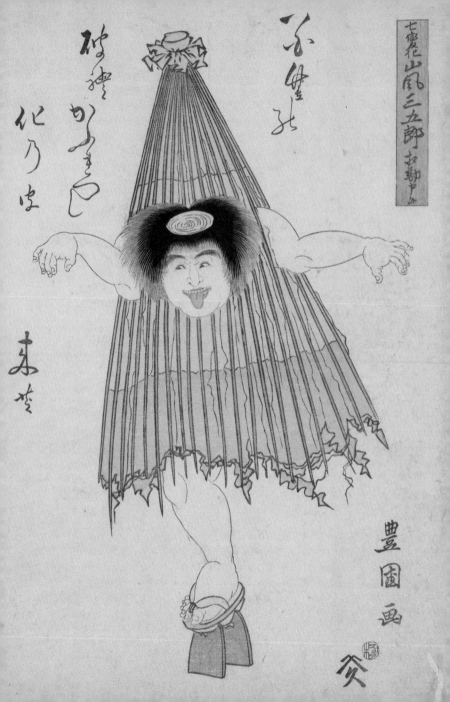

The umbrella yokai—known variously as *karakasa-obake*, *kasa-obake* or *kasa-bake*—is one of a large cast of characters that were drawn, painted and handed down over generations right through to the present day. The first known depictions appear on picture scrolls of the Edo period (1603–1868)—most notably the *Hyakki Yagyo*, or *Night Parade of One Hundred Demons*. Here, the kasa-obake takes humanoid form, with two arms, two legs, a walking stick and a goblinesque face partially enclosed by a parasol, handle forward, closed canopy sweeping backwards like beehived hair, a few wispy broken ribs escaping the cloth tied around its middle. Like a fairytale, the scroll was widely copied, referenced and retold, and different versions of the demons proliferated: other kasa-obake are depicted with the canopy open over its head like a hat, or a scarf swaddling the pointed tip like a turban, or the parasol forming the entirety of the head, with the handle beaklike: a goblin bird.

Over time, as printing technologies advanced and the woodblock print was introduced, expensive hand drawn picture scrolls were supplanted by affordable prints. An established cast of characters—amongst them, the umbrella—began to appear on anything yokai-themed, and the kasa-obake found its most iconic form: an upright parasol with one leg protruding from the closed canopy, its foot clad in a *geta* sandal, arms thrown wide for balance, one or two eyes staring unblinkingly forwards and a large open mouth, often with a long, red tongue lolling facetiously about.

Such playful beings feature on *sugoroku* boards (a board-and-dice game of the Edo and Meiji periods), on children's card games, in Kabuki plays, on glow-in-the-dark stickers and decals of the Shōwa period, and, more recently, on posters for such films as *The Great Yokai War* and *Tokaido Obake Dochu* (*Ghosts Journey the Tokaido Highway*).[27] In the Meiji period, little mechanical box toys

---

27 In one of the most stunning scenes from the 1994 Studio Ghibli film *Pom Poko* (directed by Isao Takahata), the *Night Parade of One Hundred Demons* is reenacted on a grand scale through the streets of Tokyo—including appearances from several mischievous kasa-obake.

called *kokeshi* dolls were manufactured in Kobe—one such toy features a kasa-obake that, on turning a lever, leaps from a basket and frightens a wooden figurine, whose jaw drops in astonishment.

As centuries passed and the images proliferated, the kasa-obake went the way of many yokai: they became familiar, even cute. Their disturbing and malevolent qualities dropped away, and today their role is little more than what Meech describes as "comic-book spook." Remove the comic-book context, however, and they could now be read as a kind of late-capitalist haunting: imagine if all the dumped umbrellas, mattresses, lamps, bikes, dishwashers, wardrobes, cutlery sets and thousands upon millions of other sundries were to come to life and wreak mischievous havoc upon humanity.

In becoming sentient, however, the kasa-obake also serves as an apt illustration of another aspect of umbrellaness: that in which the umbrella transcends its usual use and form to serve other purposes entirely.

7 ‖ THE BROLLY TRANSCENDENT

ONE OF THE endearing features of Dickens's "umbrella work" is the number of uses to which he put his brollies. As we have seen, they are rarely merely umbrellas but the signifiers of something else, whether through similarity, metaphor or context. In addition to a vast array of sexual clues and cues, John Bowen has found Dickensian brollies masquerading as "weapons and shields . . . birds, cabbages and leaves." And whether they're in the right place or the wrong place (like the umbrella in Quilp's eulogy), there is some intangible but undeniable facet of umbrellaness that has captured the human imagination for centuries. Perhaps it is the awkward elegance of them—these beautiful objects that are useful for so little else, that break so pathetically, that are cumbersome and accident-prone whether discarded, spread or folded. Perhaps it is their potential to arrest us, visually. Even in 1855, when the colours available for umbrella canopies were fewer and less varied than ours today, William Sangster wrote joyfully of

OPPOSITE: Poster advertising 'Revel' umbrellas, 1922

the wide, uncovered market-place of some quaint old German town during a heavy shower, when every industrial covers himself or herself with the aegis of a portable tent, and a bright array of brass ferrules and canopies of all conceivable hues . . . flash on the spectator's vision.

In *100 Essays I Don't Have Time to Write* (2014), American playwright Sarah Ruhl explores the use of umbrellas on stage and the visual satisfaction they afford the audience. She believes it is the umbrella's metaphorical power (the same power Winnie-the-Pooh appealed to with his bees) that gives it a unique ability to bestow verisimilitude on the fictive universe of the set:

The illusion of being outside and being under the eternal sky is created by the real object. A metaphor of limitlessness is created by the very real limit of an actual umbrella indoors . . . The umbrella is real on stage, and the rain is a fiction . . . A real thing . . . creates a world of illusory things.

As with theatre, so too with cinema. Movies are riddled with umbrella shots crafted by cinematographers unable to resist their appeal. *The Umbrellas of Cherbourg* (1964) opens with an extended bird's-eye view of rain spattering a pavement, umbrellas passing to and fro. An iconic shot from *Singin' in the Rain* (1952) shows Gene Kelly swinging from a lamppost, the folded brolly in his hand joyfully disregarded. Audrey Hepburn holds a gorgeous parasol aloft at the races in *My Fair Lady* (1964). And so on. Even just limiting myself to the films I watched the week I drafted this chapter, two brollies leap to mind: a stunning moment in Takeshi Kitano's film *Zatoichi* (2003) where an overhead shot of a rain-splattered roof edge gives way to the flowering of a battered red rice paper umbrella from below; or in Alfonso Cuarón's *Harry Potter and the Prisoner of Azkaban* (2004), where, before a particularly stormy quidditch match, an umbrella tumbles high through the air like a clumsy leaf.

Maybe it is the sheer irreplaceability of the umbrella that appeals. For all our leaps in technological development over the past few decades, for all our smart fridges and driverless cars and washing machines that reorder detergent online for us before we run out, there is no virtual substitute for the brolly. As Charlie Connelly says, "You can't download an app to replace the umbrella." Just as the new-fangled brollies of the industrial age were an anachronism in Sangster's "quaint old German town," so too are today's umbrellas, for the opposite reason: for all the fabrics and technologies available to us now, the basic appearance, function and design of the umbrella has changed very little in the past 150 years. And until their design is revolutionized, or some manner of keeping the rain off us without

In 2005, Slovenian artist Matej Andraž Vogrinčič suspended one thousand umbrellas in the atrium of Melbourne's former GPO building. Seen from below, the umbrellas formed a fluid, multidomed ceiling; from above, a rolling landscape of spoked black hills. From time to time a cloud of mist would drift across the installation, creating the fleeting illusion of being out-of-doors on a busy, drizzly day.

a portable roof is conceived of and mass-marketed, that doesn't look likely to change any time soon.

Whatever the reason for their enduring appeal, the imaginative possibilities of the brolly are not limited to art, theatre and the cinema: writers, too, have made full use of its shape and form throughout history. This chapter will be devoted to those instances of umbrellaness that transcend the umbrella's everyday form and function: from boats to flying machines; from clubs to swords; from umbrellas that become human (almost) to humans who (almost) become umbrella.

In his essay "Umbrellas," Dickens asks,

> Would M. Garnerin have astonished the denizens of St. Pancras, by alighting among them in a parachute liberated from a balloon, half a century ago?—would he have had many imitators, successful and unsuccessful, at all sorts of Eagles and Rosemary Branches and Hippodromes?— and, lastly, would Madame Poitevin, the only real, genuine Europa of modern times, have dropped down from the clouds on an evening visit to Clapham Common?— would all these events have occurred if umbrellas had never been invented?

The answer is, very likely, no. Today's parachutes are almost unrecognizable as umbrella-children, but in fact it was the sheer unmanageability of the umbrella in windy conditions that caught the imaginations of late-eighteenth-century aeronauts, and the object played a vital role in the development of the parachute. When William Sangster was writing *Umbrellas and Their History*, the design of the parachute commonly in use at the time was "nothing more or less than a huge Umbrella."

That's not to say that European brolly aficionados were the first

A VIEW OF MONS.ᴿ GARNERIN'S BALLOON AND PARACHUTE.

1 | The Balloon.
2 | The Pilot Balloon.
3 | The Parachute.

By which he ascended from the Volunteers Ground, North Audley Street, Grosvenor Square, Sep.ᵗ 21. 1802. to the height of 8000 Feet.
And the Parachute he descended by in a Field near S.ᵗ Pancras Church, quite safe.

4 | The Basket with M.ʳ Garnerin's
5 | Ten letters fixed to the Balloon.

Published Oct.ᵗ 22. 1802. by G. Thompson. N.ᵒ 43 Long Lane West Smithfield London.

Garnerin's balloon and umbrella-chute

to think of it; just as the Continent lagged sorely behind the rest of the world on umbrella uptake, so they did on the parachute. The Chinese *Shih Chi*, completed in 90 B.C.E., tells the story of Ku-Sou, who is trying to kill his son, Emperor Shun. Ku-Sou lures his son to a tower, then sets it alight; Shun escapes by tying several conical umbrella-hats together and leaping to safety. A late-seventeenth-century Siamese monk amused the royal court by jumping from great heights with two umbrellas fixed to his belt. Word of this reached Joseph-Michel Montgolfier, who in 1779 pushed a sheep in a basket from a high tower. The sheep floated to the ground unharmed with the aid of a seven and a half foot parasol Montgolfier had fastened to the basket. In 1838 John Hampton went even further and constructed a parachute shaped like an umbrella fifteen feet in diameter. He took it up to nine thousand feet and cut it—along with himself—loose. He landed safely after a thirteen-minute descent.

A more complete—and occasionally gruesome—record of parachute developments to 1855 may be found in William Sangster's book, of which an entire chapter is devoted to the aeronautic advances inspired by umbrellas. I, however, will move on, pausing only to note the sweet serendipity of the relationship between the two—for, as Cynthia Barnett reminds us, that which umbrellas protect us from also takes parachute form:

> We imagine that a raindrop falls in the same shape as
> a drop of water hanging from the faucet, with a point-
> ed top and a fat, rounded bottom. That picture is upside
> down. In fact, raindrops fall from the clouds in the shape
> of tiny parachutes, their tops rounded because of air pres-
> sure from below.

OPPOSITE: Czech children learn the risks of using umbrellas as parachutes in this illustration from a 1936 issue of *La Tribuna Illustrata*.

It is a logical imaginative step from umbrellas-as-parachutes to umbrellas-as-flying-machines—a step most famously made by P. L. Travers in *Mary Poppins*. The 1964 movie may have featured Julie Andrews drifting down Cherry Tree Lane in its opening scenes, but the Banks children must wait until the very end of the first book before they witness the hidden powers of Poppins's parrot-headed brolly—and a sad scene it is:

> Down below, just outside the front door, stood Mary Poppins, dressed in her coat and hat, with her carpet bag in one hand and her umbrella in the other . . . She paused for a moment on the step and glanced back towards the front door. Then with a quick movement she opened the umbrella, though it was not raining, and thrust it over her head.
>
> The wind, with a wild cry, slipped under the umbrella, pressing it upwards as though trying to force it out of Mary Poppins' hand. But she held on tightly, and that, apparently, was what the wind wanted her to do, for presently it lifted the umbrella higher into the air and Mary Poppins from the ground. It carried her lightly so that her toes just grazed along the garden path. Then it lifted her over the front gate and swept her upwards towards the branches of the cherry trees in the Lane.
>
> "She's going, Jane, she's going!" cried Michael, weeping . . .
>
> Mary Poppins was in the upper air now, floating away over the cherry trees and the roofs of the houses, holding tightly to the umbrella with one hand and to the carpet bag with the other . . .
>
> With their free hands Jane and Michael opened the window and made one last effort to stay Mary Poppins' flight.

The iconic Poppins

"Mary Poppins!" they cried. "Mary Poppins, come back!"

But she either did not hear or deliberately took no notice. For she went sailing on and on, up into the cloudy, whistling air, till at last she was wafted away over the hill and the children could see nothing but the trees bending and moaning under the wild west wind.

While umbrellas were suggesting parachutes to aeronauts, they were suggesting sails to mariners. An umbrella was incorporated into the prototype for the inflatable rubber life raft in 1844—along with a paddle, it was intended for propulsion and steering. In 1896 the "umbrella rig" was developed for use on sailing boats:

> [T]he sail when spread had precisely the appearance of a large open umbrella, the mast of the boat forming the stick. Twice as much canvas could thus be carried as by any other form of rig, and the sail had no tendency to heel the boat over.

Evidently sail-making technology superseded the umbrella-form, for the umbrella rig has quietly disappeared into the annals of sailing history[28]—although it is tempting to wonder if it wasn't a predecessor to the modern-day spinnaker.

On the subject of mariners, it takes only the smallest step of the imagination to flip the brolly upside down and turn its surface area and water-resistant qualities to advantage in repelling water from below, rather than above. A small step for man, perhaps—but a giant leap for a Bear of Very Little Brain. In the story "In which Piglet is Entirely Surrounded by Water," Winnie-the-Pooh and Christopher Robin receive a message in a bottle from Piglet, who is trapped in his house by rising floodwaters. They need a boat to rescue him, but Christopher Robin does not own a boat:

> And then this Bear, Pooh Bear, Winnie-the-Pooh, F.O.P. (Friend of Piglet's), R.C. (Rabbit's Companion), P.D. (Pole Discoverer), E.C. and T.F. (Eeyore's Comforter and Tail-finder)—in fact, Pooh himself—said something so clever that Christopher Robin could only look at him with mouth open and eyes staring, wondering if this was really the Bear of Very Little Brain whom he had known and loved so long.
>
> "We might go in your umbrella," said Pooh.

---

28 Not, however, from the annals of kayaking history, where umbrellas continue to be used to assist on long paddles, or while fishing. Anglers still make use of the "umbrella rig"—an umbrella-like structure hung with an arrangement of lures designed to look like a school of small fish.

"?"

"We might go in your umbrella," said Pooh.

"??"

"We might go in your umbrella," said Pooh.

"!!!!!!"

For suddenly Christopher Robin saw that they might. He opened his umbrella and put it point downwards in the water. It floated but wobbled. Pooh got in . . . "I shall call this boat The Brain of Pooh," said Christopher Robin, and The Brain of Pooh set sail forthwith in a south-westerly direction, revolving gracefully.

These curious craft are not limited to children's storybooks: In *The Sunshade, the Glove, the Muff* (1883), Octave Uzanne comments on sketches that may be found in albums of Japanese art, depicting

some human being excited to a singular degree, with hair tossed by the wind, and haggard eye, floating at the will of the tumultuous waves on a Parasol turned upside down, to the handle of which he clings with the energy of despair.

Umbrellas also have a long (and violent) history of being used as weapons. One early adaptation was the umbrella sword stick—a brolly with a slim sword concealed in its post. Although illegal today, they were once enough in demand to appear on James Smith & Sons's stained-glass windows—where they remain to this day.

Perhaps the most famous umbrella-related murder occurred, appropriately enough, in London. In 1978, Georgi Markov, a dissident writer from Bulgaria, was waiting for a bus by Waterloo Bridge when he felt a sharp pain in his leg. He looked behind him to see a man with an umbrella get into a car and drive away.

Within days Markov was dead, killed by a minute pellet of ricin injected into his leg by—detectives surmised—the tip of a modified umbrella. Although no arrests were made over his murder, it was thought to have been committed in connection with the Bulgarian secret police. Charlie Connelly notes that when the Bulgarian government fell in 1989, "a stock of umbrellas modified to fire tiny darts and pellets was found in the interior ministry building."

Anyone more than passingly acquainted with DC's Batman comics will be familiar with The Penguin, or Oswald Chesterfield Cobblepot, one of Batman's long-term nemeses and wielder of an extravagant array of weaponized umbrellas—amongst them, the Bulgarian design used to murder Markov. The Penguin's umbrellas include a vast range of modifications, limited only by the writer's imagination: knives, swords, guns and poison gas all make regular appearances.

One completely novel approach to umbrellas as weapons is that taken by Rubeus Hagrid, whose umbrella is far more than it initially seems. Let's return to that memorable scene on Mr Potter's eleventh birthday, when Hagrid tells Harry he's a wizard and has been invited to study magic at Hogwarts School of Witchcraft and Wizardry. Uncle Vernon roundly insults not just Harry and his parents, but the headmaster of Hogwarts as well—an insult Hagrid does not take lightly:

> He brought the umbrella swishing down through the air to point at Dudley—there was a flash of violet light, a sound like a firecracker, a sharp squeal and next second, Dudley was dancing on the spot with his hands clasped over his fat bottom, howling in pain. When he turned his back on them, Harry saw a curly pig's tail poking through a hole in his trousers ...

A magic umbrella? Not quite. The true state of affairs is revealed the next day when Hagrid takes Harry shopping for a wand at Ollivander's:

> "But I suppose they snapped [your wand] in half when you got expelled?" said Mr Ollivander, suddenly stern.
>
> "Er—yes, they did, yes," said Hagrid, shuffling his feet. "I've still got the pieces, though," he added brightly.
>
> "But you don't use them?" said Mr Ollivander sharply.
>
> "Oh, no, sir," said Hagrid quickly. Harry noticed he gripped his pink umbrella very tightly as he spoke.

However, umbrellas can inflict quite enough damage without the aid of concealed swords, poison-pellet mechanisms or magic wands. A somewhat less infamous umbrella murder occurred in 1814, in what came to be known as the "Battle of the Umbrellas" in Milan. As Nigel Rogers reports in *The Umbrella Unfurled* (2013), following the collapse of Napoleon's empire, Giuseppe Prina, a finance minister who had imposed severe taxes on the populace to meet the emperor's demands, was dragged out of the Senate by an angry mob and clubbed to death with umbrellas.

Unfortunately for Prina it was probably not the swiftest of deaths, and it was undoubtedly painful—but still not as grotesque as this Yiddish curse of uncertain provenance, which contains the most visceral umbrella violence you're ever likely to encounter: "May a strange death take him! May he swallow an umbrella and it should open in his belly!"

A late-nineteenth-century self-defense manual entitled *Broad-Sword and Single-Stick* contained an entire section on umbrellas. Echoing the sentiments of many a brollyphile indignant at the object's poor standing in society, the author writes:

> As a weapon of modern warfare this implement has not been given a fair place. It has, indeed, too often been spoken of

with contempt and disdain, but there is no doubt that, even in the hands of a strong and angry old woman, a gamp of solid proportions may be the cause of much damage to the adversary.

The authors advise deploying the umbrella in two ways—as a fencing foil (light, parrying stabs with one hand), and a bayonet (firmly grasped and thrusted with two hands).

The mad woman in *Elizabeth Is Missing* seems rather to have gone for the "club" approach in this scene, when she chases a young Maud down the street:

> . . . was holding the groceries against my chest, waiting for a tram to pass, when suddenly there was a great bang! on my shoulder. My heart jumped and my breath whistled in my throat. The end of the tram was trundling away at last, when bang! she hit me again. I leapt across the road. She followed. I ran up my street, dropping the tin of peaches in panic, and she chased me, shouting something I couldn't catch . . . There was a bruise on my shoulder for weeks after that, dark against my pale skin. It was the same colour as the mad woman's umbrella, as if it had left a piece of itself on me, a feather from a broken wing.

Just as Derrida has described the umbrella as both feminine and phallic, so too does it function as both weapon and defense. An open umbrella can act as a shield against not only rain and sun, but also bullets and other projectiles. At least two notable leaders have employed fortified umbrellas in their defense: Queen Victoria, who had a number of parasols lined with chain mail following an assassination attempt, and French president Nicolas Sarkozy, who in 2011 had a £10,000 Kevlar-coated umbrella made for his bodyguards in case of their needing to shield him. Apparently this umbrella was so strong that his bodyguards were able to smash tables with it.

Rather more outlandish is this anecdote from colonial India, related by William Sangster, in which an umbrella is put to an entirely novel defensive use:

> The members of a comfortable picnic party were cosily assembled in some part of India, when an unbidden and most unwelcome guest made his appearance, in the shape of a huge Bengal tiger. Most persons would, naturally, have sought safety in flight, and not stayed to hob-and-nob with this denizen of the jungle; not so, however, thought a lady of the party, who, inspired by her innate courage, or the fear of losing her dinner—perhaps by both combined seized her Umbrella, and opened it suddenly in the face of the tiger as he stood wistfully gazing upon brown curry and foaming Allsop. The astonished brute turned tail and fled, and the lady saved her dinner.

And her life, presumably.

One umbrella, deployed in the fateful seconds before U.S. president John F. Kennedy was fatally shot on November 22, 1963, continues to intrigue conspiracy theorists to this day. Louie Steven Witt, dubbed the "Umbrella Man," was captured on film holding an umbrella aloft moments before shots were fired at the president's car. Josiah "Tink" Thompson—one of the first to spot the Umbrella Man in footage—included Witt and his umbrella in his 1967 book *Six Seconds in Dallas: A Micro-Study of the Kennedy Assassination.* Given that the shooting occurred on a bright, sunny day, and no one but Witt was carrying rain gear of any kind, sinister theories proliferated. One suggested that the umbrella was itself a weapon used to fire a disabling dart into Kennedy's throat. Another held that the raising and lowering of Witt's umbrella functioned as a signal to the shooter(s).

John Updike, reflecting on Thompson's book in a December 1967 issue of *The New Yorker*, wrote:

> [The Umbrella Man] dangles around history's neck like a fetish . . . We wonder whether a genuine mystery is being concealed here or whether any similar scrutiny of a minute section of time and space would yield similar strangenesses—gaps, inconsistencies, warps, and bubbles in the surface of circumstance.

Despite the microanalytic nature of his own book, Thompson himself appears to agree with Updike: in Errol Morris's 2011 short film *Who Was the Umbrella Man?* Thompson states that he accepts Witt's own explanation, which he gave before the House Select Committee on Assassinations in 1978. Witt claimed that his black umbrella was raised as a protest, not at John F. Kennedy himself but his father, Joseph P. Kennedy, who in his role as U.S. ambassador to the United Kingdom had supported Neville Chamberlain in his much-hated policies of appeasement towards Nazi Germany. Thompson says, "I read that and I thought, 'This is just whacky enough it has to be true!'"

The iconicity of Chamberlain's umbrella had no doubt faded somewhat by 1963—but from a purely brolliological perspective Witt's explanation certainly checks out. However, hundreds of commenters on the video's YouTube page beg to differ, and over fifty years later, Witt's umbrella remains an object of speculation and intrigue.

On a lighter note, umbrellas also make rather handy hiding places—and not just for one's own self. In Hergé's Tintin book *The Calculus Affair* (1960), the absentminded professor Cuthbert Calculus develops a glass-shattering sonic invention that he fears could be turned into a weapon. Seeking advice, he heads for Switzerland to consult with a colleague but is abducted on the way. Tintin and Captain Haddock begin pursuit. On their hunt, they

come across the professor's signature umbrella, which Tintin's dog, Snowy, takes responsibility for, carrying it around in his mouth. When they finally intercept Calculus the first thing he asks after is "My umbrella! My umbrella!"—before he is reabducted and whisked away.

They lose his umbrella before rescuing him a final time, and there is a high-speed pursuit involving tanks and gunfire. Totally oblivious to Death flying about their ears, Calculus asks, "My umbrella! Have you got my umbrella?"—To which Captain Haddock expostulates, "Blistering barnacles, your umbrella! This is a fine time to worry about an umbrella!" However, the object is eventually recovered, prompting what is perhaps the most blissful human-umbrella reunion scene in literary history; Calculus clasps the object to his chest, crying, "My umbrella! My own little umbrella! At last I've found you!" All is explained when Calculus reveals that he had hidden the plans for his inventions inside the hollow handle of his brolly.

Hagrid's wand and The Penguin (and possibly the Umbrella Man) aside, these are all fairly quotidian examples of brollies transcending their usual designated functions. Far more boundary

Umbrella Sprite, from *Memoirs of an Umbrella*

crossing are the imaginative uses to which they have been put by writers—or hallucinogens. In *The Prime of Life* (1960), the second volume of her memoirs, Simone de Beauvoir relates Jean-Paul Sartre's first experiment with mescaline—an experience that, oddly enough, includes an umbrella or two:

> Late that afternoon, as we had arranged, I telephoned Sainte-Anne's, to hear Sartre telling me, in a thick, blurred voice, that my phone call had rescued him from a battle with several devil-fish, which he would almost certainly have lost . . . He had not exactly had hallucinations, but the objects he looked at changed their appearance in the most horrifying manner: umbrellas had become vultures, shoes turned into skeletons, and faces acquired monstrous characteristics, while behind him, just past the corner of his eye, swarmed crabs and polyps and grimacing Things.

Other monstrous associations crop up in Sarah Perry's *The Essex Serpent*: firstly, when a young girl has a vision of the titular serpent as "a coiled snake unfolding wings like umbrellas," and later when a very large and very dead sea creature washes up on the shore:

> All along the spine the remnants of a single fin remained: protrusions rather like the spokes of an umbrella between which fragments of membrane, drying out in the easterly breeze, broke and scattered.

One extraordinarily transformative brolly may be found in G. H. Rodwell's *Memoirs of an Umbrella*. As mentioned earlier, this umbrella so transcends its object status that it has become sentient and narrates a storyline of typically Victorian complexity from its (or rather, his: the umbrella is unambiguously gendered) vantage point as he is lost, loaned and forgotten, passed from character to character, "taken up here, or put down there, or dropped from a coach-box, or hung upon a peg." As the umbrella himself points out, what better perspective could be gained but that of an umbrella?

> Whether it be spread out cold, wet and weeping in the servants' hall, or, dry and snug in the butler's room; whether it be enviously watching over the heads of two happy lovers; or stuck almost upright, beneath the arm of the Honourable E. B—: still they are all situations for observing human nature.

It is a perspective that does not come cheap, according to this umbrella:

> Talk of slavery! what can be more perfect than that of an Umbrella! At one moment our tyrant masters will

Memoirs of an Umbrella: the narrator

raise us up to the skies; at the next, lower, nay, thrust us into the very mire! It is true we have . . . our moments of sunshine, but they are "few, and far-between": perhaps, the fewer the better for our well-being, for bad weather suits us best. And that, which generally makes others low, causes the umbrella to be elevated.

We learn that, while entirely dependent on humans for carriage from place to place, this umbrella has emotions and hopes and desires of his own. He is frequently irritated by being removed from all the action—"I have generally been annoyed by being carried away exactly at the very moment I had wished to stay"—and at one point he wonders, "If a poor umbrella could feel this, what ought not real flesh and blood to have felt?" Although he cannot physically move, his emotional peaks come tantalisingly close, with descriptions like, "my very silk began to tremble" and, "the name vibrated through my whalebones." Above all—for all the talk of slavery—he delights in being useful:

> We had scarcely reached the New Road when it began
> to rain, not much, certainly, but enough to raise me con-
> siderably in my own estimation . . . The rain ceasing as
> suddenly as it had commenced, I was lowered, and felt
> myself no longer of any consequence.

The central conceit of *Memoirs of an Umbrella* is ridiculous by
most standards, and it is a tribute to the author that the final work
is sufficiently compelling to draw a reader—well, this reader, at
any rate—through to the final pages. That said, sentience in brole
lies is not limited to out-of-print nineteenth-century fiction, or kasa-
obake. The Japanese poet Yosa Buson penned a haiku in which
the sentience of two inanimate objects forms the final, delightful
twist:

> *The spring rain—*
> *telling stories to each other they pass by:*
> *raincoat and umbrella.*

English Poet Denise Riley, in her poem "Krasnoye Selo," refers
to umbrellas and their "carriers" going about their daily duties—a
breathtaking reversal in which it is the umbrella that takes centre
stage, the umbrella that possesses volition. The individuals beneath
them factor in only as brolly-bearers, as enablers—not unlike the
Greek and Egyptian slaves charged with holding umbrellas over the
heads of their rulers.

Perhaps the most fascinating transcendence of all is that between human and brolly—one of which Will Self is a master. It is
Audrey—symbolic throughout this book of the anxieties connected
with the mechanical age—who undergoes this extraordinary transt
formation, not once but twice. The first time occurs just before her
encephalitis permanently relapses, when, caught in a sudden gust of
wind, Audrey's arms:

fly up and away, struts jerkily unfolding from ribs, then
bending back on themselves, so that the riveted pivots
bend and pop . . . her stockings are half unrolled on her
stiff posts, her handles in their worn leather boots rattle
across a cellar grating...

Her temporary identification with the umbrella is prophetic, for
Audrey will soon, like a broken brolly, be abandoned and all but forgotten as she succumbs to an illness no one can understand or treat,
and is shut up in a psychiatric hospital for the rest of her life.

Will Self does not quite have a monopoly on human-umbrella con-
fusions, however: the character of Miss Hare, in Patrick White's 1961
novel *Riders in the Chariot*, undergoes a comparable, although much
subtler, transformation of her own. Miss Hare, one of the four "vision⸱
aries" of the novel, is herself a creature of margins and transient boundaries: this passing comparison—introduced very early in the novel—is
a most fitting introduction to the transcendent nature of her character:

> Miss Hare continued to walk away from the post office,
> through a smell of moist nettles, under the pale disc of the
> sun. An early pearliness of light, a lambs'-wool of morn-
> ing promised the millennium, yet, between the road
> and the shed in which the Godbolds lived, the burnt-
> out blackberry bushes, lolling and waiting in rusty coils,
> suggested that the enemy might not have withdrawn. As
> Miss Hare passed, several barbs of several strands at-
> tached themselves to the folds of her skirt, pulling on it,
> tight, tight, tighter, until she was all spread out behind,
> part woman, part umbrella.

Coda ‖ BROLLYLESSNESS

IN LONDON'S BARBICAN CENTRE, over the winter of 2012–
2013, it rained. Artists Hannes Koch, Florian Ortkrass and Stuart
Wood (known collectively as Random International), transformed
the Barbican's Curve gallery into a one hundred square meter
rainstorm. Titled *Rain Room*, the free exhibition was immensely
popular—waiting times could reach eight hours—and it went on to
feature at New York's Museum of Modern Art later that year.

A constant, indoor rainstorm, carefully constructed to mimic the
look, sound and humidity of a steady downpour, is feat enough—
but the *Rain Room* went far beyond this. Highly attuned sensors
built into each sprinkler were able to detect the presence of a person
beneath them and instantly shut off—making it possible to navi-
gate the entire field without once getting wet. Of course, you had
to go gently—the sensors were not quick enough to respond to very
sudden movements or a racing child—but that is to miss the point
entirely.

The experience of shelteredness without a shelter is extraordinary and almost uncanny. It first strikes you when, standing on the

OPPOSITE: *Rain Room*, Barbican Centre, London, 2012–2013

edge, you extend a hand to test the downpour—and your hand does not get wet. Wandering through is not unlike the feeling of walking in the rain with an umbrella—except that the rain is much closer, yet you cannot touch it, cannot reach out to catch a drop. The only thing standing between you and a soaking is you yourself. It is the physical manifestation of John Donne's "we are therefore our own umbrella": you become gradually aware that you are enveloping and protecting yourself, simply by virtue of existing.

There is something very powerful about this reminder of your own physicality, something that brings to mind the reverence accorded kings and the symbolic safety net of their canopies. It's not so easy to feel protected and secure in this day and age, and it is both startling and strangely affirming—within the microcosm of twenty minutes spent walking through a small gallery space—to discover a means of shelter within yourself.

And yet . . . rain is a force that humanity has lived with since our earliest days. Over hundreds of thousands of years we have adapted our environment, our clothes, our shelters and our cities to divert, channel and catch the rain. Scientists suggest that our very bodies evolved in response to rainfall—that the pruney wrinkles which appear on our fingertips after a long soaking assisted our early ancestors in gripping slippery tree branches while climbing in inclement weather. Rain is a useful daily reminder that we cannot control the world around us, but that we belong to it.

And amid the wonder and beauty of the *Rain Room*—the soothing sound of a downpour, the dark, curved space with white lights cutting obliquely through the deluge—as your body persists in remaining dry, you begin to experience a detachment from the world: an unsettling feeling of what it must be like to be a ghost—to have a form and not be able to affect or interact with your immediate surrounds.

Because an umbrella is a means of controlling our most immediate environment. It is an exercise of choice, an intervention in circumstance. To put up an umbrella is to say: thank you, but I would rather not.

For all that, though, the umbrella remains a creature of the margins, useless in all but the wet and the hot, and thus, commonly, forgotten. And so we notice the umbrella most when we are without one—when we cannot intervene between ourselves and the sky.

This is often cast as a Bad Thing. Returning one last time to Self's *Umbrella*, we find Dr Zachary Busner in a vulnerable moment, his unsheltered mental state emphasized by his lack of physical protection in a rainshower:

> If I was that dapper chap on the telly, he thinks, I'd've
> brought my umbrella with me. But he is none of these
> things: dapper, a chap, on the telly—and so arrives . . .
> hunched over, his sports coat sodden, his grey flannel
> trousers greyer.

There is a lovely umbrella-nuance early in Thomas Hardy's short story "The Three Strangers" (1883). In this story, the strangers of the title all seek shelter in a remote house on a wild, blustery night, described thus:

> The level rainstorm smote walls, slopes and hedges . . .
> while the tails of little birds trying to roost on some scraggy
> thorn were blown inside-out like umbrellas.

In a clever little gesture, the birds' tails (inside-out) serve to emphasize that the kind of shelter they allude to is sorely lacking for all three characters.

But is umbrellalessness always such a terrible thing? In Herman Melville's *Moby-Dick* (1851) a character's state of umbrellalessness is cast as a sign of hardiness—"peculiar" perehaps, but hardy nonetheless:

Yes, it was the famous Father Mapple . . . He had been a
sailor and a harpooner in his youth, but for many years
past had dedicated his life to the ministry. At the time
I now write of, Father Mapple was in the hardy winter
of a healthy old age . . . No one having previously heard
his history, could for the first time behold [him] without
the utmost interest, because there were certain engraft-
ed clerical peculiarities about him, imputable to that ad-
venturous maritime life he had led. When he entered I
observed that he carried no umbrella, and certainly had
not come in his carriage, for his tarpaulin had run down
with melting sleet, and his great pilot cloth jacket seemed
almost to drag him to the floor with the weight of the
water it had absorbed.

The erotic potential of sharing an umbrella has been, I think,
well documented; that of not using one at all, perhaps less so. In
Hiromi Kawakami's 2001 novel *The Nakano Thrift Shop*, the main
character's blossoming affection towards her coworker Takeo is del-
icately hinted at in her awareness of his rain-soaked skin:

[Takeo] had gone out without an umbrella. When he came
back, he was soaking wet. Mr Nakano tossed him a towel
. . . The strong smell of the rain wafted from Takeo's body.

A memory, Brisbane, 2010: A friend and I were sitting in a café when the hot, high summer sky closed over.
The sticky air gave way to dark purpling clouds and a
cool, keen wind. The chirring cicadas fell suddenly silent.
Distant rumbles tumbled closer as lightning split the sky.
As we paid, the earth sighed: droplets plummeted, in
handfuls at first, then in buckets, spilling off the tarmac,
runnelling through gutters, pummeling trees. We stepped
outside into the scent of it. Waiting the storm out was not

an option; I was running late, and my car was parked at my friend's house. So we ran, dashing from tree to tree at first, and then, as the fat drops hit our hair, our faces, and soaked our clothes in seconds, we gave up and walked: sodden, delirious, exhilarated. It was an experience that transcended the possibilities of an umbrella. We did not have one—nor, that day, would we have wanted one.

Oddly enough, I started writing this book because—until recently—I did not like using umbrellas. Getting rained on has never bothered me: I have always preferred a thorough soaking to a dry torso and a pair of wet ankles, or the awkward huddling scuttle of sharing an umbrella with others. It comes, I suppose, of a childhood spent someplace warm, where the air is kind on a damp body, where you can run outside and feel the wild excesses of the weather through your skin without risking pneumonia.

But I have always loved umbrellas—for their elegance of form and function, for their pathetic comic sweetness in defeat. When I moved to England I learned some important lessons about Warmth, and one of them was Not Gallivanting About in the Rain. And the more I hunted umbrellas from book to book, throughout history and up and down the streets of London, the more I came to appreciate them: for their wonderful cosiness amid the chill and drizzle, for their many symbolisms and rich cultural diversity, for their humble interventions in those moments when you think to yourself: No, I would really rather not.

ACKNOWLEDGEMENTS

I F IT TAKES a village to raise a child, it took an intercontinental conglomerate of family, friends and publishing experts to get this book out into the world. I owe deep thanks to the many people who supported me, my manuscript or both over the past few years. In particular:

To this book's very first readers, Gillian Rankine, Peter Rankine and Jake Murray, who dutifully read a scratchy chapter every week and responded with nothing less than lively interest, love and encouragement. Mum, for that big old gold umbrella shading your baby lettuces. Papa, for your wonderful thoughts on form.

And to its next readers: Sally Molloy, Amy Austin, Phil Walsh and Rachel Walker. Thank you for your gentle suggestions, pages of handwritten notes, historical guidance, and home-cooked meals.

To Jonathan Ruppin, for your unstinting advice, feedback and support on all matters books and publishing.

To everyone at Melville House involved in editing, design and production, especially Dennis Johnson and Valerie Merians, Nikki Griffiths, Susan Rella, my editor Ryan Harrington (unfailingly helpful and an incredibly thoughtful reader) and designer Marina Drukman, who transformed an ugly Word document into something truly stunning. *Brolliology* couldn't have been in better hands.

To my beautiful husband, Jake: woof to my quack, interstellar co-adventurer, and the only person I have ever known capable of outwitting my prodigious aptitude for procrastination.

To the Brolly Hunters—all the family, friends and colleagues who shared their favourite umbrella stories, photos, artworks, music, films and literary encounters, and in doing so, helped shape this book.

And finally, to Bydie, who could not be here to read it, but without whom many, many wonderful things would not have been possible.

ENDNOTES

1. MARKS OF DISTINCTION

11   **"must be reckoned an umbrella"**: cited in T. S. Crawford, *A History of the Umbrella*.

11   **"seven chiefs had been killed"**: ibid.

12   **"in the sun or in the shade"**: ibid.

12   **"carried for his shadow but him"**: ibid.

13   **warlord Wang Kuang, dated to 25 B.C.E."**: Nigel Rodgers, *The Umbrella Unfurled: Its Remarkable Life and Times*.

14   **sturdy paper umbrellas instead**: Crawford.

14   **"threw themselves upon our Chausseurs"**: cited in Crawford.

15   **"And his umbrella too!"**: ibid.

22   **"hurry, temper . . . carelessness"**: cited in Ariel Beaujot, Victorian Fashion Accessories.

27   **"I fairly exploded with laughter"**: cited in Crawford.

27   **"the unfortunate consequences of colonialism"**: Matthew Solomon, *Fantastic Voyages of the Cinematic Imagination: George Melies's Trip to the Moon*.

28   **"democratic versus despotic"**: Beaujot.

2. DISREPUTABLE OBJECTS

32   **"umbrellas of taffeta or waxed silk"**: cited in Crawford.

32   **"a wetting."**: ibid.

34   **"one possesses no carriage"**: cited in Crawford.

34   **"get a coach, Monsieur?"**: ibid.

40   **"what proceeded from dirt"**: cited in William Sangster, *Umbrellas and Their History*.

3. SHELTER, SHADOW, SHIELD

57   **"our own umbrella and our own suns"**: cited in Crawford.

59   **"those who seek shelter under him"**: ibid.

60   **the very act of sheltering him**: Cynthia Barnett, *Rain: A Natural and Cultural History*.

60   **occasionally include umbrellas**: Rodgers.

66   **"flywhisks and parasols"**: cited in Rogers.

67   **that of quotidian sunshade**: Crawford.

68   **"make clear her path ahead"**: cited in Crawford.

70   **"insteps with her umbrella"**: cited in Bowen.

70   **"shoulders with her umbrella"**: ibid.

70   **"gained you for my wife"**: cited in Beaujot.

4. THE GENDERED BROLLY

76   **the "bed" of a dissecting table**: Man Ray, L'Enigme d'Isidore Ducasse.

79   **"as do women"**: cited in Crawford.

79   **"consider them effeminate"**: ibid.

80   **"the behest of a nagging landlady"**: cited in Barnett.

80   **"welcome to the maid's pattens"**: cited in Crawford.

82   **"how many intoxicating and magic looks?"**: cited in Rodgers.

83   **"another weapon of coquetry"**: cited in Beaujot.
83   **"the sunshade that she carries in her hand"**: ibid.
84   **bright colours on display**: Crawford.
85   **"the exhibitions of an eccentric appendage"**: cited in
      Crawford.

5. A HAT WITH A HANDLE

90   **and she holds up a parasol**: Crawford.
93   **"They go inward and move inward"**: cited in Barnett.

6. FORGOTTEN OBJECTS AND FRIGHTFUL MORALITIES

119   **"BOOKS, UMBRELLAS, AND MONEY!"**: cited in Sangster.
120   **"members of his joint-stock home"**: cited in Beaujot.
121   **"robbers never carry umbrellas"**: cited in Crawford.

7. THE BROLLY TRANSCENDENT

135   **and leaping to safety**: Crawford.
138   **"the sail had no tendency to heel the boat over"**: from *The
      Mariner's Mirror*, vol. 34, quoted in Crawford.
141   **"and it should open in his belly!"**: Benjamin Harshav, *The
      Meaning of Yiddish*.
141–142 **"may be the cause of much damage to the adversary"**: cited in
      Charlie Connelly, *Bring Me Sunshine*.

CODA: BROLLYLESSNESS

154   **while climbing in inclement weather**: Barnett.

ILLUSTRATION CREDITS

Image 1: Woman sits with parasol
Unattributed illustration in *The Sphere*, June 11, 1927. Copyright
Illustrated London News Ltd/Mary Evans Picture Library.

Image 2: Advertisement for the London Underground, 1929 (colour litho)
Manner (fl.1920s). Private Collection, DaTo Images/Bridgeman Images.

Image 3: Bijutsu Kei [Ocean of Art]
Vol. 1, 1904, woodblock print. Courtesy Special Collections Division,
Newark Public Library, Newark, NJ.

Image 4: Advertisement for Fox's Umbrellas, 1901
Advertisement in *The Illustrated London News*, January 12, 1901, and
September 7, 1901. Copyright Illustrated London News Ltd/Mary
Evans Picture Library.

Image 5: Fresco from the Gupta Empire
Ajanta fresco paintings second century B.C.E. to sixth century C.E.
Reprinted from https://en.wikipedia.org/wiki/Umbrella#/media/File:
Ajanta_Paintings.jpg.

Image 6: Ornamental State Umbrella, with Silver Handle, India
Print, 1851, from Art & Picture Collection, New York Public Library,
Astor, Lenox and Tilden Foundations.

Image 7: Caricature of Prince George, Duke of Cambridge
Cartoon by Alfred Bryan, *The Entr'Acte*, July 16, 1881. Copyright Terry
Parker/Mary Evans Picture Library.

Image 8: Umbrellas in The Pen Shoppe, Brisbane
Photo by author.

Image 9: Hanway's Umbrella
Engraving by an unnamed artist. From Mary Evans Picture Library.

Image 10: Sarah Gamp
Illustration by KYD—Joseph Clayton Clarke in the 1880s. From Mary
Evans Picture Library.

Image 11: Sky-Striker and Shield-Bearer
Reprinted from J. S. Duncan, *Hints to the Bearers of Walking Sticks and
Umbrellas* (London: J. Murray, 1809).

Image 12: Inverter and Mud-Scooper
Reprinted from J. S. Duncan, *Hints to the Bearers of Walking Sticks and
Umbrellas* (London: J. Murray, 1809).

Image 13: Mr Tumnus and Lucy
Illustration by Pauline Baynes copyright C. S. Lewis Pte Ltd 1950, taken
from *The Lion the Witch and the Wardrobe* by C. S. Lewis C. S. Lewis
Pte Ltd 1950. Reprinted by permission.

Image 14: Keep Dry
Packaging, transportation and receiving symbol: keep dry. Reprinted
from https://commons.wikimedia.org/wiki/File:Keepdry.svg.

Image 15: Nut, Geb and Shu
From Wallis Budge, *Gods of the Egyptians*, vol. 2, p. 96. Reprinted from
Mary Evans Picture Library.

Image 16: Night Flight
Illustration by Pauline Baynes copyright C. S. Lewis Pte Ltd 1950, taken
from *The Lion the Witch and the Wardrobe* by C. S. Lewis copyright C. S.
Lewis Pte Ltd 1950. Reprinted by permission.

Image 17: A king's grave in Central Africa
From Mrs Fanny E. Guinness, *The New World of Central Africa. With a
History of the First Christian Mission on the Congo . . . with Maps . . . and
Illustrations* (London: Hodder & Stoughton, 1890). Courtesy of the
British Library.

Image 18: Woman holding an umbrella, eighth century B.C.E.
Print, 1851, from Art & Picture Collection, New York Public Library,/
Astor, Lenox and Tilden Foundations.

Image 19: *Two Couples (Lovers)*
Woodblock print by Kitagawa Utamaro, Edo period. Courtesy of
Special Collections Division, Newark Public Library, Newark, NJ.
Courtesy Special Collections Division, Newark Public Library.

Image 20: Umbrella jump
Suzuki Harunobu, 1725–1770, *Young Woman Jumping from the Kiyomizu*

Temple Balcony with an Umbrella as a Parachute, Edo period, 1765 (Meiwa 2). Photograph copyright 2017 Museum of Fine Arts, Boston.

Image 21: *Correspondence of Rajomon*
Suzuki Harunobu, *Correspondence of Rajomon*, 1770. From Mary Evans Picture Library/Library of Congress.

Image 22: A procession of suffragists
Postcard published by Miller & Land. Copyright The March of the Women Collection / Mary Evans Picture Library.

Image 23: Sunshades for 1909
Illustration in *The Throne and Country*, vol. 4, May 15, 1909, p. 322. From Mary Evans Picture Library.

Image 24: *Travelers in the snow*
Woodblock print by Katsushika Hokusai, Edo period. Special Collections Division, Newark Public Library, Newark, NJ. Courtesy Special Collections Division, Newark Public Library.

Image 25: Robinson Crusoe
Unattributed engraving from Mary Evans Picture Library.

Image 26: Hemlock, or poison parsley
Illustration by Mabel E. Step, in Frederick Step, *Wayside and Woodland Blossoms*, p. 85. From Mary Evans Picture Library.

Image 27: Parasol interior
Photo by author.

Image 28: I think this one exploded?
Photo by author.

Image 29: Flower behind the ear, Liverpool
Photo by author.

Image 30: Gutter monster, London
Photo by author.

Image 31: Broken blossom
Photo by author.

Image 32: Dalek
Photo by author.

Image 33: Mr Liston as Paul Pry
Appleton, William Worthen, Mr. Liston as Paul Pry. Collection of theatrical correspondence and ephemera/Series II: Portraits/Sub-series 2—Twopence coloured, n.d. Print. Billy Rose Theatre Division, New York Public Library for the Performing Arts, Astor, Lenox and Tilden Foundations.

Image 34: Umbrella ghost
Utagawa Toyokuni, the actor Arashi Sangoró III as an umbrella ghost, photo. Copyright Herbert Boswank. Reproduced with permission, Kupferstich-Kabinett, Staatliche Kunstsammlungen, Dresden.

Image 35: Poster advertising "Revel" umbrellas, 1922 (colour litho)
Cappiello, Leonetto (1875–1942), Private Collection. Copyright Ackermann Kunstverlag/Bridgeman Images.

Image 36: Umbrellas in Melbourne's former GPO Building
When on a Winter's Day a Traveller, installation by Matej Andraž Vogrinčič, 2005. Photo copyright Hyland Leslie Harvey. Reproduced with permission.

Image 37: Garnerin's parachute
Published by G. Thompson, Long Lane, West Smithfield, London.
Copyright The Royal Aeronautical Society (National Aerospace
Library)/Mary Evans Picture Library.

Image 38: Parachutes (or not . . .)
Illustration by Vittorio Pisani in *La Tribuna Illustrata*, September 20,
1936. From Mary Evans Picture Library.

Image 39: Mary Poppins
Reprinted by permission from HarperCollins Publishers Ltd. Copyright
1934 P. L. Travers/Mary Shepard.

Image 40: My Umbrella!
From Hergé, *The Calculus Affair*. Reprinted by permission of Editions
Casterman copyright Hergé/Moulinsart 2016.

Image 41: Umbrella sprite:
From George Herbert Rodwell, *Memoirs of an Umbrella* (London: E.
MacKenzie, 1845). Illustrations by Landells, from designs by Phiz.

Image 42: The narrator
Illustrations by Landells, from designs by Phiz. From George Herbert
Rodwell, *Memoirs of an Umbrella* (London: E. MacKenzie, 1845).

Image 43: Rain Room
By Random International, Curve, Barbican Centre, 2012–2013.
Photo by author.

WORKS CITED AND CONSULTED

Agualusa, José Eduardo. *A General Theory of Oblivion*. Translated by Daniel Hahn. London: Vintage, 2016.

Atwood, Margaret. *The Blind Assassin*. 2000. Reprint. London: Virago, 2008.

Austen, Jane. *Persuasion*. 1816. Reprint. Middlesex: Penguin Books, 1965.

Barnett, Cynthia. *Rain: A Natural and Cultural History*. New York: Crown, 2015.

Beaujot, Ariel. *Victorian Fashion Accessories*. London: Berg, 2012.

Bowen, John. "Dickens's Umbrellas." In *Dickens's Style*, edited by Daniel Tyler, 26–45. Cambridge: University of Cambridge Press, 2013.

Cannadine, David. "Neville Chamberlain's Umbrella." *Prime Ministers' Props*. BBC Radio 4. London: 103–105 FM. August 10, 2016.

Carey, John. *The Violent Effigy: A Study of Dickens' Imagination*. 1973. Reprint. London: Faber & Faber, 1991.

Carver, Lou. "Top This . . . The Story of Top Hats." *Victoriana Magazine*. Accessed August 12, 2016. http://www.victoriana.com/Mens-Clothing/tophats.htm.

Chesterton, G. K. *The Innocence of Father Brown*. 1911. Reprint. London: Penguin Books, 1950.

Connelly, Charlie. *Bring Me Sunshine*. 2012. Reprint. London: Abacus, 2013.

Crawford, T. S. *A History of the Umbrella*. Devon: David & Charles, 1970.

Dahl, Roald. "The Umbrella Man." In *Collected Stories of Roald Dahl*, 796-802. London: Everyman's Library, 2006.

De Beauvoir, Simone. *The Prime of Life*. Translated by The World. 1960. Reprint. Middlesex: Penguin Books, 1965.

Defoe, Daniel. *Robinson Crusoe*. 1719. Reprint. Oxford: Oxford University Press, 1998.

De Lautréamont, Comte. *Les chants de maldorer*. Translated by Alexis Lykiard. Cambridge: Exact Change, 1994.

Derrida, Jacques. *Spurs: Nietzsche's Styles*. Translated by Barbara Harlow. Chicago: University of Chicago Press, 1979.

Dickens, Charles. *Martin Chuzzlewit*. 1843. Reprint. London: Penguin Classics, 1986.

Dickens, Charles. "Mr Minns and His Cousin." 1833. Charles Dickens Page. Accessed October 31, 2015. http://charlesdickenspage.com/mr_minns_and_his_cousin.html.

Dickens, Charles. "Please to Leave Your Umbrella." *Household Words* 17 (1858): 457–59.

Dickens, Charles "Umbrellas." *Household Words* 6 (1853): 201.

Duncan, J. S. *Hints to the Bearers of Walking Sticks and Umbrellas*. London: J. Murray, 1809.

Flaubert, Gustave. *Madame Bovary*. Translated by Geoffrey Wall. 1992. Reprint. London: Penguin Books, 2001.

Forster, E. M. *Howard's End*. 1910. Reprint. London: Penguin Classics, 2000.

Forster, E. M. *A Room with a View*. 1908. Reprint. London: Penguin Books, 1978.

Gardiner, A. G. "On Umbrella Morals." English in CCE. Accessed October 24, 2014. http://www.englishincce.in/2014/05/on-umbrella-morals.html.

Greene, Graham. *The End of the Affair*. 1951. Reprint. London: Vintage Classics, 2012.

Hardy, Thomas. "The Three Strangers." 1883. East of the Web. Accessed

February 23, 2016. http://www.eastoftheweb.com/short-stories/UBooks/ThreStra.shtml.

Harshav, Benjamin. *The Meaning of Yiddish*. Berkeley: University of California Press, 1990.

Healey, Emma. *Elizabeth Is Missing*. London: Viking, 2014.

Hergé. *The Calculus Affair*. Translated by Leslie Lonsdale-Cooper and Michael Turner. 1960. Reprint. London: Egmont, 2012.

Kafka, Franz. *Amerika*. Translated by Edward Muir. New York: New Directions, 1962.

Kang, Han. *The Vegetarian*. Translated by Deborah Smith. London: Portobello Books, 2015.

Kawakami, Hiromi. *The Nakano Thrift Shop*. Translated by Allison Markin Powell. London: Portobello Books, 2016.

Kirby's Wonderful and Scientific Museum, or, Magazine of Remarkable Characters. Vol. 2. London: R.S. Kirby, 1804.

Köhler, Stephen. "Parents of Private Skies." In Julia Meech, *Rain and Snow: The Umbrella in Japanese Art*. New York: Japan Society, 1993.

Koichi, Yumoto. *Yokai Museum*. Translated by Pamela Miki Associates. Tokyo: PIE International, 2013.

Kundera, Milan. *The Unbearable Lightness of Being*. Translated by Michael Henry Heim. London: Faber and Faber, 1985.

Kureishi, Hanif. "The Umbrella." In *Collected Stories*. London: Faber and Faber, 2010.

Lewis, C. S. "It All Began with a Picture . . . " In *On Stories: And Other Essays on Literature*. Orlando: Harcourt, Inc., 1982.

Lewis, C. S. *The Lion, the Witch and the Wardrobe*. 1950. Reprint. London: Collins, 1998.

Mantel, Hilary. *The Giant, O'Brien*. London: Fourth Estate, 1998.

Meech, Julia. *Rain and Snow: The Umbrella in Japanese Art*. New York: Japan Society, 1993.

Melville, Herman. *Moby-Dick; or, The Whale*. 1851. Reprint. London: University of California Press, 1979.

Milne, A. A. *Winnie-the-Pooh*. 1926. Reprint. London: Mammoth, 1989.

Mullan, John. "Ten of the Best . . . Brolleys." *The Guardian*. September 18, 2010. Accessed March 23, 2013. https://www.theguardian.com/books/2010/sep/18/10-best-brolleys-in-literature.

Park, Ruth. *The Harp in the South*. 1948. Reprint. London: Penguin Classics, 2001.

Perry, Sarah. *The Essex Serpent*. London: Serpent's Tail, 2016.

Poole, John. *Paul Pry: A Comedy, In Three Acts*. New York: E. M. Morden, 1827.

Ray, Man. *L'Enigme d'Isidore Ducasse*. Tate exhibit 1972. Accessed September 29, 2016. http://www.tate.org.uk/art/artworks/man-ray-lenigme-disidore-ducasse-t07957.

Riley, Denise. "Krasnoye Selo." In *Say Something Back*. London: Picador, 2016.

Rodgers, Nigel. *The Umbrella Unfurled: Its Remarkable Life and Times*. London: Bene Factum, 2013.

Rodwell, George Herbert. *Memoirs of an Umbrella*. London: E. MacKenzie, 1845.

Rowling, J. K. *Harry Potter and the Philosopher's Stone*. 1996. Reprint. London: Bloomsbury, 2001.

Ruhl, Sarah. *100 Essays I Don't Have Time to Write*. New York: Farrar, Straus and Giroux, 2014.

Sangster, William. *Umbrellas and Their History*. 1855. Reprint. Editora Griffo, 2015.

Self, Will. *Umbrella*. London: Bloomsbury, 2012.

Sewell, Brian. *The White Umbrella*. London: Quartet, 2015.

Shaw, George Bernard. *Pygmalion: A Romance in Five Acts*. 1913. London: Penguin Classics, 2000.

Shorter Oxford English Dictionary. 6th edition. 2 vols. Oxford: Oxford University Press, 2007.

Solomon, Matthew. "Introduction." In *Fantastic Voyages of the Cinematic Imagination: George Melies's Trip to the Moon*, edited by Matthew Solomon, 1–24. New York: State University of New York Press, 2011.

Stevenson, Robert Louis. "The Philosophy of Umbrellas." 1894. In

Quotidiana. Edited by Patrick Madden. March 24, 2007. Accessed November 1, 2013. http://essays.quotidiana.org/stevenson/philosophy _of_umbrellas.

Travers, P. L. "Mary Poppins." In *The Mary Poppins Omnibus*, 11–222. Leicester: Carnival, 1999.

Turfa, Jean M. "Parasols in Etruscan Art." *Notes in the History of Art* 18, vol. 2 (1999): 15–24.

Uzanne, Octave. *The Sunshade, the Glove, the Muff.* London: J. C. Nimmo and Bain, 1883.

Watson, Norman. "Text and Imagery in Suffrage Propaganda." 2007. Scottish Word and Image Group. Accessed February 7, 2017. http: //www.scottishwordimage.org/debatingdifference/WATSON.pdf.